GW00507435

CONTEM

General Editors
MALCOLM BRADBURY
and
CHRISTOPHER BIGSBY

# V. S. NAIPAUL

## IN THE SAME SERIES

# V. S. NAIPAUL

## PETER HUGHES

ROUTLEDGE
LONDON AND NEW YORK

First published in 1988 by
Routledge
a division of Routledge, Chapman and Hall
11 New Fetter Lane, London EC4P 4EE

Published in the USA by
Routledge
a divison of Routledge, Chapman and Hall, Inc.

Typeset by Rowland Phototypesetting Ltd
Printed in Great Britain by
Cox and Wyman Ltd, Reading, Berks.

British Library Cataloguing in Publication Data
Hughes, Peter, 1940–
V. S. Naipaul 1.—(Contemporary writers).
1. Fiction in English. Trinidadian writers
(Vidiadhar Surajprasad). Naipaul, V.S.,
1932–
I. Title    II. Series
813

ISBN 0-415-00654-6

Library of Congress Cataloging in Publication Data
Hughes, Peter, 1940–
V. S. Naipaul/Peter Hughes.
p.   cm.—(Contemporary writers)
Bibliography: p.
ISBN 0-415-00654-6 (pbk.)
1. Naipaul, V. S. (Vidiadhar Surajprasad), 1932–   —Criticism and
interpretation.   I. Title.   II. Series.
PR9272.9.N32Z74 1988
823'.914—dc19      88-15772 CIP

*To Joanne and in memory of George*

# CONTENTS

# GENERAL EDITORS' PREFACE

The contemporary is a country which we all inhabit, but there is little agreement as to its boundaries or its shape. The serious writer is one of its most sensitive interpreters, but criticism is notoriously cautious in offering a response or making a judgement. Accordingly, this continuing series is an endeavour to look at some of the most important writers of our time, and the questions raised by their work. It is, in effect, an attempt to map the contemporary, to describe its aesthetic and moral topography.

The series came into existence out of two convictions. One was that, despite all the modern pressures on the writer and on literary culture, we live in a major creative time, as vigorous and alive in its distinctive way as any that went before. The other was that, though criticism itself tends to grow more theoretical and apparently indifferent to contemporary creation, there are grounds for a lively aesthetic debate. This series, which includes books written from various standpoints, is meant to provide a forum for that debate. By design, some of those who have contributed are themselves writers, willing to respond to their contemporaries; others are critics who have brought to the discussion of current writing the spirit of contemporary criticism or simply a conviction, forcibly and coherently argued, for the contemporary significance of their subjects. Our aim, as the series develops, is to continue to explore the works of major post-war writers – in fiction, drama and poetry – over an international range, and thereby to illuminate not only those works but also in some degree the artistic, social and moral assumptions on which they rest. Our wish is that, in their very variety of approach and emphasis, these books will stimulate interest in and understanding of the vitality of a living literature which, because it is contemporary, is especially ours.

*Norwich, England*

MALCOLM BRADBURY
CHRISTOPHER BIGSBY

# PREFACE AND ACKNOWLEDGEMENTS

For some years now, and in all the notes on the author published in his books, V. S. Naipaul has taken to closing the remarks about where and when he began to write with the statement, 'He has followed no other profession.' The sentence has the dry pride of something that might have been said by Samuel Johnson and the poise of everything written by Naipaul. It has the added merit of being true. He is one of the very few writers of our time who has always and only lived by his work. And he has *followed* his profession in a quite literal sense: ever since he left Trinidad in his teens to come to England, he has been 'travelling to write'. Not only to write his novels and stories, but also to compose the enquiries into remote places and pasts, books such as *An Area of Darkness*, *The Loss of El Dorado*, and *Among the Believers* that are something more than travel narratives or narrative history. They are kinds of writing that have, as we shall see, a deep and tangled relation to his fiction, a twinned relation that in his most recent book, *The Enigma of Arrival*, has become almost Siamese. This brief study of his work begins by suggesting why we should read all of his writing together as a life's work. It is a life decided by writing and dominated by visions of a world undoing itself; visions that arise out of the writing and reading he has made into his world.

His vision of disorder and decline has often been considered a kind of malice, especially by those subjects of past or passing empires, British or American, French or even Belgian, who have felt themselves mocked; or by believers who find themselves attacked as superstitious. But that overlooks the obsessed origins and literary development of his visions. He cast around for a theme, which then cast itself around him. Before he could even understand the impotence and rawness of his boyhood colonial world, he had read about Rome, the crises of the Republic, the long fall of the Empire. Gibbon before him had cast around for a theme, something to write about, and even thought that his great work would be entitled *The History of the Liberty of the Swiss*. Imagine Gibbon without irony; for that is a subject that would not survive much irony, praising the sturdy faith of their pastors, the crusts and curds that nourished their liberty, and you will be able to imagine how fortunate he and we all have been that he 'sat musing amidst the ruins of the Capitol' for the idea of his *Decline and Fall* to come to him. As with Gibbon, so with Naipaul, whose ironic vision of the world is comparable to the historian he echoes in *The Mimic Men*. Above all because the writing out of the narrative of decline and fall, of disorder and the loss of authority, involves – as Lionel Gossman has piercingly said of Gibbon – the 'discovery of a void at the heart of the world'.[1] Such a void lies at the heart of Naipaul's world, and it has been discovered through his writing.

His own biographical history has long had a symbiotic and self-consuming relation with that writing. His work at first consumed his life, which has over time come to envelop and dissolve the formal patterns of his writing. All biographical facts are selected details of larger fictions, and the way such facts are combined shows what sort of story they are meant to tell. A glance at the biographical note that appears in all the Penguin editions of Naipaul's books, for example, tells us the bare facts of a recycled life: 'V. S. Naipaul was born in Trinidad in 1932. He came to England in 1950 to do a university course, and began to write, in London, in 1954. He has followed no other profession.' Then follows a paragraph of titles, publication dates, and prizes. The note closes with a paragraph that shows how the relation between life and work began to change, how the recycling began:

In 1960 he began to travel. *The Middle Passage* (1962) records his impressions of colonial society in the West Indies and South America. *An Area of Darkness* (1964) is a reflective and semi-autobiographical account of a year in India. *The Overcrowded Barracoon* (1972) is a selection of his longer essays, and *India: A Wounded Civilization* (1977) is an extended study – prompted by the 1975 Emergency – of Indian attitudes. His latest novel is *A Bend in the River*.

This note to a 1980 reprint of *The Mimic Men* is at once assertive and reticent. It offers a life that will account for the later writing after erasing the earlier life and rewriting it as fiction.

It also passes over in silence and ellipses many of the biographical facts we might expect to see tabulated in a *Who's Who* entry or a *curriculum vitae*. Such a note might begin very differently; as follows, for example:

Vidiadhar Surajprasad Naipaul was born in Chaguanas, Trinidad in 1932, educated there at the Queen's Royal College and at University College Oxford, after which he went down to London in 1954 to begin his career as a writer. In 1955 he married Patricia Ann Hale. His publications include *The Mystic Masseur* (1957), *The Suffrage of Elvira* (1958).

Such an entry would tell us several things suppressed in the Penguin note, starting with the Hindu given names there masked by terse initials. We also learn that Naipaul had an élitist education in Trinidad (unmentioned in the note) that was continued in England ('to do a university course' understates his undergraduate years at Oxford to the point of concealment). The date of his marriage and name of his wife would be given in such an entry, but the givens here outline an absence in his work. This absence calls attention to itself, becoming a virtual presence; the more self-centred and reflexive his work becomes, the more this silence becomes audible.

12

The traditional and imperial bias of such an entry, which usually recounts in tabular form the triumphs of the generals and directors-general, the OM and the Grand Old Man, conceals the colonial abyss out of which Naipaul scrambled, suppresses the exotic poverty of his early life, the thread of ink his life hung on until a scholarship pulled him up and away to Oxford. And just as the self-portrayal of *The Enigma of Arrival* omits any reference to a wife, the autobiography of his early life, told in *Finding the Centre* and in a number of essays, omits all but the most glancing references to his years at Oxford. What Naipaul's recycled and interlaced writer's life reveals and conceals is the circularity of interpretation itself. Not a vicious circle, but rather a spiral of understanding: 'You cannot travel on the path,' says Gautama Buddha, 'before you have become the Path itself.'

Part of that discovery has been the uncovering of his own Hindu and Brahmin ancestry. His travels to India bring home to the reader and to him the hold of taboo, the longing for purity and dread of defilement that had come down to him out of what he calls 'a bottomless past'. This descent may or may not be a genetic code of sorts, but it becomes I think part of another code, part of the heightened awareness of violation that runs through his work. His writing touches on other codes or ways of presenting the world: romantic prose to present the English countryside, which he at times sees as Uganda or Trinidad, transformed by his writing; anthropologists' and travellers' accounts of places he is writing about himself; the code of understatement and ellipsis in modern fiction as a necessary way to convey a vision of excess and chaos.

Throughout this life of writing Naipaul insists that what he aims at is not fantasy or triumphs of the imagination – all of which he discounts and dismisses – but truth to his own experience, which in turn defines him as a writer. He would I think agree with Wallace Stevens that the imagination is always 'at the end of an era'. And Naipaul might also agree that such an end is the writer's moment, his beginning: 'It is not that there is a new imagination, but that there is a new reality.'[2] And in the new reality conveyed by Naipaul's writing, literature

13

transcends distinctions between fiction and nonfiction to become once again what it was in the time of Gibbon and Johnson, and what it may become again: all writing of quality with a claim to permanence.

I should like to express my thanks to colleagues and students at the University of Zürich who questioned and commented on my first attempts to discuss what became this book; to Jacqueline Good, Hortensia von Roten, Eugene Trubowitz and above all, to Fritz Gutbrodt.

# A NOTE ON THE TEXTS

Page references for quotations from V. S. Naipaul's writings are to the British Penguin editions unless otherwise indicated. The following abbreviations have been used:

| | |
|---|---|
| SE | *The Suffrage of Elvira* |
| MS | *Miguel Street* |
| HMB | *A House for Mr Biswas* |
| MP | *The Middle Passage* |
| SKC | *Mr Stone and the Knights Companion* |
| AD | *An Area of Darkness* |
| FI | *A Flag on the Island* |
| MM | *The Mimic Men* |
| LED | *The Loss of El Dorado* |
| IFS | *In a Free State* |
| OB | *The Overcrowded Barracoon* |
| IWC | *India: A Wounded Civilization* |
| G | *Guerrillas* |
| REP | *The Return of Eva Perón* with *The Killings in Trinidad* |
| ABR | *A Bend in the River* |
| AB | *Among the Believers* |
| FC | *Finding the Centre* |
| EA | *The Enigma of Arrival* (London and New York: Viking, 1987) |
| AG | Seepersad Naipaul, *The Adventures of Gurudeva* (London: André Deutsch, 1976) |
| NYRB | *New York Review of Books* |

# 1

## A WORLD UNDOING ITSELF

After the leaves have fallen, we return
To a plain sense of things. It is as if
We had come to an end of the imagination,
Inanimate in an inert savoir.

It is difficult even to choose the adjective
For this blank cold, this sadness without a cause.
The great structure has become a minor house.
No turban walks across the lessened floors.
(Wallace Stevens, 'The Plain Sense of Things')

Toward the end of *The Enigma of Arrival*, Naipaul's narrator recounts some private events and visits (to London for 'a prize-giving lunch', to his dentist for the dismaying extraction of a molar – 'a sense of death' – the search for a new flat); but the public world breaks in on him.

> Then Mrs Ghandi was shot dead by her bodyguard in Delhi. Immediately after that there was a visit to Germany for my publisher in that country: the shock of East Berlin, still in parts destroyed after forty years, seedlings grown into trees high on the wrecked masonry of some buildings, a vision of a world undoing itself: new to me: I should have gone long before to look. (*EA*, p. 310)

This glimpse of the world beyond the Wall excites the narrator's sense that here too there is a void, a world devolving through history toward dereliction and loss. But the loss is not irrevocable. Naipaul might be said to revoke it through what he writes. Not so much because trees grow out of the ruins: nature's victories over culture, Congo hyacinths that choke the river's channel, even English ivy strangling a cherry tree are to

17

Naipaul stages in the world's undoing that he dates as precisely as battles or catastrophes.

In an essay on Zaire that offers as history what later becomes fiction in the novel *A Bend in the River* (1979) Naipaul writes in 1975 of

> a water plant that appeared on the upper Congo in 1956 and has since spread all the way down, treacherously beautiful, with thick lily-like green leaves and a pale-lilac flower like a wilder hyacinth. It seeds itself rapidly; it can form floating islands that attract other vegetation; it can foul the propellers of the steamer. If the steamers do not fail, if there are no more wars, it is the Congo hyacinth that may yet imprison the river people in the immemorial ways of the bush. ('A New King for the Congo. Mobutu and the Nihilism of Africa', *REP*, p. 177.)

In *The Enigma of Arrival*, a book that assumes a knowledge of his life and work that few writers could assume, Naipaul attempts what he calls 'a synthesis of the worlds and cultures that made me'. Although called a novel, it more resembles what François Mauriac wrote and called a *mémoire intérieure*. It is a work that spirals outward into the world from the author's Wiltshire cottage, upward into daylight from the dream of fear in an ancient seaport figured in a painting by de Chirico whose title becomes the title of the book. The interlaced lives and fates of Naipaul, his reclusive landlord, and the declining estate they both inhabit, are traced through the reading of the forty-seven rings of a cherry tree finally brought low by ivy. By ivy allowed at a certain moment to run rampant:

> Here in the secret vegetable life of the cherry tree of the garden was something like confirmation of what I had heard about the life of my landlord. In 1949 or 1950 – being the year I had left my own home island, had made my roundabout journey to England, looking for material to write about, and being as a writer (in the pieces I attempted) much more knowledgeable than I was as a person, hiding myself from my true experience, hiding my experience from myself – in 1949 or 1950 my landlord had withdrawn from the

world, out of an excess of knowledge of that world. That probably was when he had given orders that the ivy was not to be touched. Up to that time the garden laid out by his parents had been more or less tended, in spite of everything, in spite of the war. Four or five years later, going by the evidence of the rings on my disc of cherry wood, the ivy had taken; and twenty-one years after that the choked, strangled tree had collapsed and became part of the debris of the garden, the debris of a life. (*EA*, p. 197)

Hyacinths spreading down the Congo, ivy coiling around the cherry tree, seedlings arching into trees above East Berlin, are all part of Naipaul's 'vision of a world undoing itself', a vision that remakes through prose a world undone by events.

I have quoted these sketches or natural histories at length because their poise and concision seem to contradict the disorder that is their argument. The repetition at the end of this last passage of 'the debris of the garden, the debris of a life' has the effect of a second fall, or even a third, because it implicates the narrator as well as his landlord; the alliterative irony with which the hyacinth 'may yet imprison the river people in the immemorial ways of the bush' is worthy of Gibbon, who is often echoed in Naipaul and who may also have inspired the double and doubting historical conditionals of 'If the streamers do not fail, if there are no more wars'; and in the closing sentence of the first passage, the 'seedlings grown into trees high on the wrecked masonry', the perfect placing of 'high' followed by the reflexive surprise of 'undoing itself' and the abruptness of the pair of colons that set off 'new to me'; all of these are tokens of Naipaul's powers and qualities as a modern and modernist writer. What I mean by modern will emerge later, but I mean by modernist this special relation between the vision of undoing and the writing that ravels up a counterpoised and ordered pattern or vision. Naipaul, for all the traditionalism of his early fiction, has since become in all his work a writer who does what the great modernists do: he makes good through style what has been lost through history.[3]

The intertwining of Naipaul's story with that of the ivy, the linking of the years of his life with the rings of the cherry tree, bring out the pattern or grain of this passage and of the book in which it appears. This is a writer's story, and his life must in great part be an enabling fiction that will allow him to write. Naipaul blurts out part of this when he aligns the year the ivy began to take over with his own decision to leave Trinidad and everything he knew to follow a life of writing. He was travelling to write, 'looking for material to write about', and the one wild thing about this colonial boy was his motiveless creativity, as mysterious in its ways as the weariness of the world and of good works he surmises in his landlord. He even aligns his own despairing attempt to engage himself in the world through writing with his landlord's withdrawal, with the accidia that is the obverse of Naipaul's ambition:

> It occurred to me one day that at the time the ivy had taken or become established on the cherry tree, at the time my landlord's accidia had become permanent, while he was still a youngish man, I would have left Oxford. And since I had to do something, and since I had left home to be a writer, and no other talent or vocation had declared itself in me, I had set myself up as a writer — as deliberately as that. There was no joy in that decision. That was the blankest and most frightening year of my life.

What begins as a vision of opposites turns to concentrate on the writer, on Naipaul, whose vision of his landlord may in its turn be an enabling fiction about and for himself. The narrator tells us more than once that he saw his landlord only twice, and that he held back from meeting or confronting him. Hence the assertion that the landlord had left the world, gone into seclusion on the estate twenty years before Naipaul moved into one of its cottages 'out of an excess of knowledge of that world', is mere surmise but wonderful symmetry. Especially since we elsewhere learn, from the same interested source, that the landlord's handful of literary attempts confirm the narrator's belief that his antitype and object of fascination has gone for the life rather than for the work. The suspense created by symmetry is further increased by the network of intermediaries who see and talk to the landlord our narrator can only envision. It is as though, in a sequel to *The Turn of the Screw*, the governess has returned to Bly years later as a middle-aged spinster and been settled in one of the cottages, just down the lane from her sometime employer, as unattainable as ever and by now past caring about the ghosts of the past. By the time the narrator comes to the estate the symmetry of desire has lost its sense of opposition. He has engaged the world through writing and, he tells the reader, 'I had come to the manor in a mood of withdrawal myself' (*EA*, p. 195). He had also *sought out* this empty cottage on its overgrown grounds where ivy, among other natural, economic and historical causes, is bringing about the undoing of the manor's and landlord's little world, whose decay begins to repeat the larger disorder that is the subject of his books set in Africa, India, South America and the West Indies.

Repetition, which comes to permeate *The Enigma of Arrival*, seeps down into its phrasing, its incidents, its themes, creating meaning through recurrence, like the allusions to literature, history, and art that run through the book. Each of these, like repetition itself, combines sameness and difference, and it is this combination that excites Naipaul's interest and deepens his narrative. The seedlings that have become trees above the durable destruction of East Berlin take Naipaul by surprise ('new to me: I should have gone long before to look') not because he has not seen anything like it before, but because he has seen and described something very like it so often before in the Third World, as this description of the obliterated Arab and Belgian past in Zaire may suggest:

> Bush has buried the towns the Arabs planned, the orchards they planted, as recently, during the post-independence troubles, bush buried the fashionable eastern suburbs of Stanleyville, near the Tshopo falls. The Belgian villas were abandoned; the Africans came first to squat and then to pillage. . . . In 1975 some of the ruins still stand, and they look very old, like a tropical, overgrown Pompeii, cleared of its artifacts, with only the ruins of the Château de Venise nightclub giving a clue to the cultural life of the vanished settlement. (*REP*, p. 183)

21

Seeing this undoing drawing closer is one of the repeated visions in *The Enigma of Arrival* and in Naipaul's work of the past few years.

Even earlier, still distanced in the darkness of Africa, this undoing is full of a sense of menace, as in the abandoned lakeside resort that is almost the end of Bobby and Linda, the two travellers whose journey makes up the action of the novella and title-story of *In a Free State*. This 'novel' consists of two other stories, which are framed along with the novella by opening and closing journal entries, purportedly transcribed from a travel diary kept by the author. Each section or story moves outward from an enclosed space – ferry boat, Washington apartment, London basement, car driving across Africa, Egyptian tourist bus – outside which the world is undoing itself. When Bobby and Linda drive into the resort, on the edge of a lake that is itself on the edge of the former Belgian Congo, everything at first looks ordinary and ordered,

> And then, quickly, the town that had looked whole showed its dereliction. The drives of villas were overgrown, disgorging glaciers of sand and dirt through open gateways. The park was overgrown. The globes and imitation coach-lamps in walls had been smashed and were empty. Metal was everywhere rusty. . . . The roofs of some villas had broken down. One verandah roof, of corrugated iron, was hanging like a bird's spread wing. (*IFS*, p. 166)

Corrugated iron is always a bad sign in Naipaul, as we shall see; but here, in this brilliant story, it is only one part that stands for a much more terrifying whole. As Bobby and Linda take a turn after dinner down one of the darkened streets, lit only by squatters' fires from the verandahs of abandoned villas, they are surrounded by first one, then several, and finally a pack of guard-dogs gone wild. They escape back to the safety of the fluorescent boulevard and the colonel's hotel, but the reversion to overgrown and savage life of what was once trained and tamed has a special horror for Naipaul. In *The Enigma of Arrival*, after the letting-go of the last of the manor's gardeners,

22

after the death of Mr Phillips, who with his wife had shored up the estate, things began to run downhill fast:

> And the people who came to work in what remained of the garden had become marauders, vandals.
>
> The very kind of people who, in the great days of the manor, would have given of their best as carpenters, masons, bricklayers, might have had ideas of beauty and workmanship and looked for acknowledgement of their skill and craft and pains, people of this very sort now, sensing an absence of authority, an organization in decay, seemed to be animated by an opposite instinct: to hasten decay, to loot, to reduce to junk. And it was possible to understand how an ancient Roman factory-villa in this province of Britain could suddenly, after two or three centuries, simply with the letting-go by authority, and not with the disappearance of a working population, crumble into ruin, the secrets of the building and its modest technologies, for so long so ordinary, lost.
> (*EA*, p. 292)

This last allusion to the end of Roman Britain is also to my mind an allusion to Conrad, a notable exception to Naipaul's lack of enthusiasm for other novelists, and in particular to Conrad's *Heart of Darkness*. This has become a mythic tale by which a vision of the world's undoing repeats and perpetuates itself: its mythic stature can be seen in Francis Ford Coppola's film *Apocalypse Now*, where it provides the story-line as well as a governing metaphor. Both the novella and Conrad's *A Personal Record*, a story repeating a travel-log in a way that parallels many of Naipaul's double narratives, haunt *A Bend in the River*. When Marlow says, in the first words he speaks, 'And this also . . . has been one of the dark places of the earth', he refers to the first rather than last days of Roman Britain, but the metaphor shifts in Naipaul toward the end from this beginning ('after two or three centuries') and the figure of darkness is what gives meaning to Naipaul's moving phrase for what it is like to live within a few miles of Stonehenge, Winchester, and Amesbury; to live for once, at last, at least for a while, within history:

23

Yet there was an uncelebrated darkness before the foundation of that town of Amesbury in 979 A.D., as recorded by the sign. More than five hundred years before that, the Roman army had left Britain. And Stonehenge had been built and had fallen into ruin, and the vast burial ground had lost its sanctity, long before the Romans had come. So that history here, where there were so many ruins and restorations, seemed to be plateaux of light, with intervening troughs and disappearances into darkness.

We lived still on one such plateau of historical light. (*EA*, p. 50)

Naipaul's vision of the world, like the mythic stature of Conrad's *Heart of Darkness*, depends upon its power to translate one history or story into others, to show that the relation between fiction and history is not the difference between falsehood and truth, but rather a distinction between converging narratives with different origins. Both fiction and history have stories to tell and repeat; both satisfy converging aspects of Naipaul's hunger to realize a world, to engage the world through writing. Hence in part the dovetailing in his work of these kinds of narrative: *The Loss of El Dorado* (1969) is history written toward the figurative truth of fiction, while *The Enigma of Arrival* takes its rise and its title from art – a painting by de Chirico – but is written toward the documentary truth of history.

What distinguishes fiction from history in Naipaul is above all this absence or presence of the document. In his Postscript to *The Loss of El Dorado* he explains, 'This narrative was structured mainly from documents – originals, copies, printed – in the British Museum, the Public Record Office, London, and the London Library. Most of the translations are my own. Dialogue occurs as dialogue in the sources' (*LED*, p. 379). What appeals to him about the eloquent and nightmarish documents that structure this visionary history of his 'own home island' is their closeness to fiction. Even more than closeness, perhaps, is their chameleon power to look like truth without the need for fantasy or novelistic tricks. Pausing over the account of Domingo de Vera, for whom the City of Gold

24

seems real and at hand precisely because of the warnings he receives — 'El Dorado was only a day away, the Indians told Vera. "Wee sayde wee would goe thither; they tolde us they were now in their *borracheras* or drunken feasts, and would kill us"' — Naipaul goes on, 'It was like proof. The legend of El Dorado, narrative within narrative, witness within witness, had become like the finest fiction, indistinguishable from truth' (*LED*, p. 38). And of course, apart from the utter delusion of it all, the intertwined narratives and witnesses that made up the legend of El Dorado were indistinguishable from truth. Like the history of witchcraft, which Norman Cohn has shown to be based on a similar and self-confirming network of documents and witnesses[4], this visionary history exceeds fiction while seeming to follow the documents. Archives and documents, whether they lie inside the Public Record Office or a Trinidad police station, are another enabling device that allows Naipaul to side-step and then go beyond the claims of fiction. Why he needs to do this is a question we will turn to in a moment, but there can be little question that the found or fabricated document underlies and as it were *underwrites* the originality of his narrative.

Two examples among many, some lines of translated verse and a few pages of a journal, show Naipaul's boldness in using discovered and invented documents. The lines of verse appear in 'Michael X and the Black Power Killings in Trinidad'; they are from Lamartine, translated by a father, a former officer who has moved from London to California, and sent in a letter to his daughter, Gale Benson, a white groupie living out political and erotic Black Power fantasies in a Trinidad commune. After Christmas and New Year's celebrations that included much feasting and sharpening of cutlasses, and possibly the drinking of blood from a slaughtered calf,

On January 2, 1972, Gale Benson was stabbed nine times, one stab going right through the base of her neck. She was buried while still alive in a four-foot hole on the bank of a ravine some two hundred feet north of Malik's house. (*REP*, p. 69)

Shortly before she was murdered, suffering the fate of a fake living among fakes with fantasies even stranger than her own, she received her father's letter. Her life and death, according to Naipaul, echoed the mutual corruption of colonist and colonizer he found most perfectly expressed by Conrad, but this time in his story 'An Outpost of Progress'. The lines of verse are prophetic of her death, which in turn fulfilled the deranged literary fantasies she naively gave her life to:

> On these white pages, where my verses unfold,
> May oft a souvenir, perchance your heart recall.
> Your life also only pure white pages behold,
> With one word, happiness, I would cover them all.
> But the book of life is a volume all sublime,
> That we cannot open, or close just at our time,
> On the page where one loves, one would wish to linger,
> Yet the page where one dies, hides beneath the finger.
>
> (REP, p. 75)

The bookishness of this whole story goes beyond the white pages and book of life named in these lines. As Naipaul observes, and with mounting force and excitement

> This was a literary murder, if ever there was one. Writing led both men there: for both of them . . . writing had for too long been a public relations exercise, a form of applauded lie, fantasy. (REP, p. 76)

and

> Like an episode in a dense novel, it served many purposes and had many meanings. And it had been devised by a man who was writing a novel about himself, settling accounts with the world, filling pages of the cheap writing pad and counting the precious words as he wrote. . . . Such plotting, such symbolism! The blood of the calf at Christmas time, the blood of Gale Benson in the new year. And then, at the end of the sacrificial day, the cleansing in the river, with Benson's surrogate pyre on the bank. (REP, pp. 88–9)

The intensity of this may owe something to the way in which this documented acting-out through writing of ignorant fantasy seems to parody, as it menacingly retells and repeats, the story Naipaul has told several times over – especially in *The Overcrowded Barracoon* (1972) and *Finding the Centre* (1984) – of his own early struggles to write himself out of ignorant fantasies about English life and fiction, neither of which he could respond to; to write himself into the sardonic and nostalgic world of the West Indies, which required not so much fantasy as the exile's total recall. This is the struggle that produced novels such as *The Mystic Masseur* (1957) and *A House for Mr Biswas* (1961), in which Naipaul also slipped out from under the weighty models of fictional realism to make do with the makeshift structures of Dickens and H. G. Wells. Wemmick's *bricolage* seems to inspire many of Naipaul's portrayals in the early West Indian fiction, and both the scope and title of *Mr Polly* can be traced in *A House for Mr Biswas*.[5] The tangled relations between Naipaul the writer and Michael X the fantasist and fanatic develop and are partly resolved in the novel *Guerrillas* (1975), to which the Michael X essay stands as a document and as an incitement. As a document it provides the written records without which this stranger-than-fiction account of a world undoing itself in Trinidad, of bodies being buried in his own backyard, might seem improbable as fiction and incredible as history. Excerpts from letters and police ledgers anchor fantasies in the historical world, which is oddly more literary than fiction in its compulsory appeal to written records. The novelist can appeal to the reader's sense of how we experience the world, to some shared notions of human nature, but the historian and his narrative are tied to records, to a second and second-hand nature out of which he has to create the illusion of a first-hand nature, until the account of how it really happened merges into an illusory proof *that* such things really happened. Even the events and facts that seem the smallest and strongest links in historical narrative have been expanded and shaped by interpretations that alone give them meaning. The decisive events in *The Killings in Trinidad*, for example, are as we have seen governed by symbols, just as the whole story is a misreading of the life of Malcolm X, in its turn a parable told for a purpose. Naipaul's exclamation,

27

'Such plotting, such symbolism!' suggests the double meaning of *plotting* and the ways in which this duplicity in the documents incites and excites him as a writer.

Above all because, as he reminds the reader, the document that as it were *underwrites* his own novel *Guerrillas* is itself foretold in the novel that Malik starts to write about himself, or about a self he sees as the object of the erotic fascination of whites, a fantasy confessed in semi-literate fiction that later becomes utterly true. Naipaul seizes on this eerie paradox, which he later made part of the narrative technique of *Guerrillas*:

> An autobiography can distort; facts can be realigned. But fiction never lies: it reveals the writer totally. And Malik's primitive novel is like a pattern book, a guide to later events. That scene of causeless tension at the house with the daughter, the wife, the retinue: just as such a scene was witnessed at Arima by a black woman visitor on the Sunday before Joe Skerritt was murdered. (*REP*, p. 67)

Set off by italics, this pattern book reappears in *Guerrillas*. This novel recounts the delusions of Roche and Jane, a pair of white liberals who come to a place that resembles both Trinidad and Guyana, and their entanglement in the politics and Black Power fantasies of Jimmy — who finally enacts that fantasy by sodomizing and killing Jane. The fictional account of *Guerrillas* retraces and cuts deeper into the symbolic patterns of Malik's writings. The pattern holds as Jimmy writes out his imagined effect on Jane, a middle-class English murderee:

> *I drive past his solitary forbidding house many times and often late at night I see the lamp burning in his study, he's wrapt up in his thoughts and I have no wish to intrude and aggravate his impatience because I know he's writing that book he has contractual obligation to write. One day I summoned up the courage to telephone him, my heart was beating when he answered, I put the phone down, though I'm dying to hear that soft and cultivated voice, that dark brown voice as it has so aptly been described by many —* (G, p. 62)

This is more fictive, more fully imagined, than the scraps from the document; hence its fuller projection of Jimmy's fantasies ('fiction never lies: it reveals the writer totally') and its use of literary clichés. Naipaul even leaves a faint spoor of the over-writing and literary reworking that has gone into this parody of romantic obsession. Jimmy's house is called 'Thrushcross Grange', and the allusion to *Wuthering Heights* is sharpened by a passage from Jimmy's lined pad, 'everybody will say then "This man was born in the back room of a Chinese grocery, but as Catherine said to Heathcliff 'Your mother was an Indian princess and your father was the Emperor of China'. . . ."' (*G*, p. 62). The spoor and paper trail left by literature across Naipaul's writings, both stories and histories, show that fiction, as he says, never lies; but it also shows that the revelations of fiction can be masked by the other and alternative mode of writing he mentions, that of autobiography.

In his career of travelling to write they have been alternate modes of writing, and the snarled relations traced here between fantasist, novelist, and historian bind together works that might seem to have come undone in ordinary literary terms. *In a Free State* is clearly great prose written out of an obsessive insight into a natural void of uncombined elements and politically 'liberated' states. All of this is implied by its title, but its contents page makes it seem an odd assemblage of two short stories and a novella, held together by a prologue and epilogue at either end. Its structure and strange unity starts to emerge once we recognize that the stories, although otherwise quite unlike one another, retell as fiction travel tales and histories that have gone into the making of Naipaul's self as a writer. It is this implied self that wrote the journal entries that stand like bookends on both sides of the stories. Both prologue and epilogue are written as though they are actual diary passages, offered to the reader as though they are extracts ('from a Journal'), parts of a writer's log that might resemble Conrad's *A Personal Record*.

*Might*, but even the existence of such a log depends on the preposition 'from' that may, like Coleridge's Preface to *Kubla Khan*, turn into fragments what should be read as two more fully told stories about the implied and actual author of the book. This relation to the writer, who reappears as the omniscient author in the novella, becomes clear if we also see and hear him behind both the Bombay servant and the West Indian fantasist who are the narrators of the two short stories. This is not so far-fetched as it may seem, especially if we relate the very different styles of the two stories to different accounts Naipaul gives of his own growth as a writer. These differences in style and narration follow from the radical distinction between one narrator and another in stories that are cast in the form of monologues. And each voice retells or records what has already been written as a document by Naipaul about his self-discovery as a writer.

The first of these, 'Tell Me Who to Kill', is written in the heightened pidgin of a West Indian worker in London. There he devotes himself to his layabout brother Dayo, who 'is pursuing his studies' without ever catching them. Like so many of Naipaul's characters, this narrator speaks out of daydreams made up of half-remembered Hollywood films – the kind that provided the fantasy life of Naipaul's boyhood – half-blind glimpses of big city life, the language of signs and educated clichés . . . and reveries of violence that recur in the endless present tense of his life's story. His dreams of revenge against white boys who torment him and make trouble in his roti shop turn into a novelistic sketch:

> Then, always, in the quiet, I see the boy's face surprised. And it is strange, because he and Dayo are college friends and Dayo is staying with him in this old-fashioned wood house in England. It is an accident; they was only playing. But how easy the knife go in him, how easy he drop. I can't look down. Dayo look at me and open his mouth to bawl, but no scream coming. He want me to help him, his eyes jumping with fright, but I can't help him now. It is the gallows for him. I can't take that for him. I only know that inside me mash up, and that the love and danger I carry all this time break and cut, and my life finish. Nothing making noise now. The body is in the chest, like in *Rope*, but in this English house. (*IFS*, pp. 96–7)

This passage, like the story it is part of, echoes the style of Naipaul's first stories and the vicarious fantasy of his early life. It also prefigures the dream made fiction and flesh in 'The Killings in Trinidad': the spiral of stories, documents, memories, and visions that create and recreate his life as a writer. It is a spiral and not a closed circle; the voices of his early stories are controlled by the narration of an implied author, but these later voices really are 'in a free state'. They have seized control of the stories they tell.

The opening sentence of 'Bogart', the first story in *Miguel Street* (1959), which although published third was the first of his books to be written, runs, 'Every morning when he got up Hat would sit on the banister of his back verandah and shout across, "What happening there, Bogart?".' And this sentence runs like a refrain through Naipaul's account in *Finding the Centre* (1984) of how he lost and found himself as a writer. In his first attempts he was writing out of ignorant fantasy about an English world he could not understand. But when, on BBC rustleproof paper and a typewriter set at single-space, he wrote that sentence, it was both the discovery of a world and his self-exposure to that world's disorder and demotic speech. His account is suggestive:

> As diarists and letter-writers repeatedly prove, any attempt at narrative can give value to an experience which might otherwise evaporate away. When I began to write about Bogart's street I began to sink into a tract of experience I hadn't before contemplated as a writer. This blindness might seem extraordinary in someone who wanted so much to be a writer. Half a writer's work, though, is the discovery of his subject. And the problem for me was that my life had been varied, full of upheavals and moves. (*FC*, p. 26)

Over time Naipaul has shown that the tracts of experience that make up his discovered subject are tractless wastes of illusion that have to be charted and envisioned. Illusion has to be turned into vision; his invention has to take control over his discovery. This is true of his fiction in ways that are both obvious and subtle. The first sentence of 'Bogart' is followed by

31

a second: 'Bogart would turn in his bed and mumble softly, so that no one heard, "What happening there, Hat?" The first sentence was true. The second was invention' (*FC*, p. 19). Naipaul seizes control through the aside 'so that no one heard', and this control of demotic disorder through Augustan and ironic prose was to mark his writing from that moment on. And yet even that is too simple; the mark is itself a spoor, because the demotic or pidgin dialogue is also Naipaul's work, as observer if not as inventor. He *makes* the world he then envisions as undoing itself.

The subtlety of this emerges as Naipaul re-emerges from India in the closing pages of *An Area of Darkness* (1964), a departure that might also serve as an arrival in the second story from *In a Free State*, 'One out of Many'. The closing paragraph of this book, ostensibly a record of his travels around India during the months that led up to the shock of the Chinese invasion in 1962, shows with great clarity the paradox that underlies Naipaul's style and its relation to his vision of a world undoing itself:

> The world is illusion, the Hindus say. We talk of despair, but true despair lies too deep for formulation. It was only now, as my experience of India defined itself more properly against my own homelessness, that I saw how close in the past year I had been to the total Indian negation, how much it had become the basis of thought and feeling. And already, with this awareness, in a world where illusion could only be a concept and not something felt in the bones, it was slipping away from me. I felt it as something true which I could never adequately express and never seize again. (*AD*, pp. 266–7)

And yet he has expressed it, not adequately but superbly; this paragraph actually creates an awareness that is said to be slipping away out of memory.

If we set this beside the superficially very different discourse of Santosh, a servant off the streets of Bombay who follows his master to Washington, we may see how deep this paradox runs; how woven it is into metaphor, which is the paradox of identity we need to talk about everything else, including the absence or loss of identity. Santosh is the eloquent narrator and unlikely hero of 'One out of Many'. His narrated experience may sound pathetic and comic: he wobbles from job to job through the flaming urban riots of the late sixties, from Hindu prejudice against blacks ('the Darks' of Aryan myth) into the embrace of a Negro woman twice his size. But the way these experiences are narrated, in lapidary prose and stoical tones, transforms his life into fate. Santosh's English, if we are to believe his own account, is so bad that he cannot follow movie dialogue, so incorrect that it can be improved by the check-out girl at the supermarket: '"Me black and beautiful" was the first thing she taught me. Then she pointed to the policeman with the gun outside and taught me: "He pig"' (*IFS*, p. 34). Santosh is also so Candide-like, so apparently sunk in a world of Hindu illusion, that he doesn't see the 'poor country weed' he has brought with him for the marijuana it is, nor the bogosity of the Hari Krishna dancers he first meets in one of Washington's landscaped traffic circles. But how can we believe him or think him simple? Santosh narrates his story in an English whose concision and elegance are utterly beyond the self that undergoes the events of that story:

> I am a simple man who decided to act and see for himself, and it is as though I have had several lives. I do not wish to add to these. Some afternoon I walk to the circle with the fountain. I see the dancers but they are separated from me as by glass. Once, when there were rumours of new burnings, someone scrawled in white paint on the pavement outside my house: *Soul Brother*. I understand the words; but I feel, brother to what or whom? I was once part of the flow, never thinking of myself as a presence. Then I looked in the mirror and decided to be free. All that my freedom has brought me is the knowledge that I have a face and have a body, that I must feed this body and clothe this body for a certain number of years. Then it will be over. (*IFS*, pp. 57–8)

This summing-up is also a summoning up of the awareness and subtlety that it denies: it is a remarkable parallel to the self-denying evocation of illusion at the end of *An Area of*

*Darkness.* The parallel between the conclusions, between the journey west and the journey east, between fiction and meditation, between the two literary paradoxes (awareness of illusion, subtlety of candour) that are created by Naipaul's masterful style, all of these parallels depend upon a shared metaphor. They might even be said to hang by the same thread.

The shared metaphor begins as the account of an experience revisioned as a dream at the end of *An Area of Darkness.* Just before flying away from India Naipaul is given a present, a parcel of cloth, by a new friend, an architect who has him promise to have it made up into a jacket in Europe. He does so, and this gift, this friendship, dominates his recollections of India. Among the streets and walls of London he feels lost and homeless. Then, he says, 'I had a dream':

> An oblong of stiff new cloth lay before me, and I had the knowledge that if only out of this I could cut a smaller oblong of specific measurements, a specific section of this cloth, then the cloth would begin to unravel of itself, and the unravelling would spread from the cloth to the table to the house to all matter, *until the whole trick was undone.* Those were the words that were with me as I flattened the cloth and studied it for the clues which I knew existed, which I desired above everything else to find, but which I knew I never would. (*AD*, p. 266)

Notice that Naipaul's account of his dream is presented through words (*'until the whole trick was undone'*, and the emphasis is his) as well as through the image of the unravelling cloth. This unravelling, which seems at first a symbol, would become an actual negation and uncreation of the universe. It would become the world undoing itself, not as a feared end; rather as a consummation to be wished. But one that would escape attainment, would always conceal the clues needed to bring it about.

Here again we notice the paradox of Naipaul's knowledge of his ignorance ('which I desired above everything else to find, but which I knew I never would'), his quietism about the end of the material world, which is belittled as a trick. The end of Santosh's story, written several years later, echoes this note of quietism and hints at the dream-metaphor of cloth and clothing: '. . . and clothe this body for a certain number of years. Then it will be over.' The hint had already been offered in his story of a green suit that is his first failed attempt to fit himself into the American world: 'The suit was always too big for me. Ignorance, inexperience; but I also remember the feeling of presumption . . . . Later I wore the pants, but never the jackets. I never bought another suit; I soon began wearing the sort of clothes I wear today, pants with some sort of zippered jacket' (*IFS*, p. 36). Clothing as renunciation, as resignation: what he is reduced to after he escapes from his employer and can no longer wear the dhoti he fashions from cloth that was his gift on leaving India.

> The urge came upon me to dress as I might have done in my village on a religious occasion. In one of my bundles I had a dhoti-length of new cotton, a gift from the tailor's bearer that I had never used. I draped this around my waist and between my legs, lit incense sticks, sat down crosslegged on the floor and tried to meditate and become still. (*IFS*, p. 39)

But this is Washington in the late sixties. What Santosh calls 'the capital of the world' is undoing itself; the alabaster city is dimmed by smoke from the fires lit by blacks.

Naipaul's vision of a world undoing itself may be related to an even stranger fable. Writing about Borges in *The Return of Eva Perón*, he dismisses most of the mystification that surrounds stories that are in his eyes 'intellectual games' or jokes. But there is one that strikes him as perfect of its kind. It purports to be a fragment from the *Voyages* of one Suarez Miranda, published in Lérida in 1658; an invention not unlike the sources for Naipaul's *The Loss of El Dorado*, though fanciful in a different way. In its entirety and brevity, and in Naipaul's version, it goes as follows:

> In that Empire, the craft of Cartography attained such Perfection that the Map of a Single province covered the space of an entire City, and the Map of the Empire itself an entire Province. In the course of Time, these Extensive maps were found somehow wanting, and so the College of Car-

tographers evolved a Map of the Empire that was of the same Scale as the Empire and coincided with it point for point. Less attentive to the Study of Cartography, succeeding Generations came to judge a map of such Magnitude cumbersome and, not without Irreverence, abandoned it to the Rigours of sun and Rain. In the western Deserts, tattered Fragments of the Map are still to be found, Sheltering an occasional Beast or beggar; in the whole Nation no other relic is left of the Discipline of Geography. (*REP*, p. 117)

This could be read as an inversion or perfect parody of a certain kind of baroque learning, but it could also be understood as a reversal of Naipaul's earlier dream of unravelling. In Borges it is the metaphor or representation, the one-to-one scale map, that first feigns the world and then is destroyed or abandoned to it. Naipaul, who may have singled this piece out because he saw or felt its closeness to his own darker thoughts, dreams of a metaphor that becomes the world and then destroys it.

There is of course a difference between the witty counterfeit of Borges and Naipaul's apocalyptic reverie. What they have in common are deep misgivings about the value of fictions and fantasies in representing the world. Despite his reputation as a mystifier, Borges is to Naipaul a great writer whose best work 'is neither mysterious nor difficult' (*REP*, p. 116). It could even be said, though Naipaul does not make this point, that the prose puzzles, which are usually read as the height of fictionality, could be read in an opposite sense as deeply subversive of fiction. Most have to be what they are, extracts and fragments from mock-books, because if they were longer they would take on the erosive and uncreating frenzy of Swift's *Tale of a Tub* or Pope's *Dunciad*. Naipaul has had from the beginning an even more special view of fantasy, an even more selective and dismissive view of novelists and works of fiction. Although he has often made this plain in articles and interviews, his dissent over the fictional canon and over the value of fiction has not been sufficiently noticed or considered. It underlies the convergence of his fictive, historical, and travel writing, and accounts in part for the originality of his work since *The Mimic Men* (1967), *The Loss of El Dorado* (1969) and *In a Free State* (1971).

36

# 2

## AN END OF THE IMAGINATION

> Yet the absence of the imagination had
> Itself to be imagined. The great pond,
> The plain sense of it, without reflections, leaves,
> Mud, water like dirty glass, expressing silence
>
> Of a sort, silence of a rat come out to see,
> The great pond and its waste of the lilies, all this
> Had to be imagined as an inevitable knowledge,
> Required, as a necessity requires.
> (Wallace Stevens, 'The Plain Sense of Things')

Growing up in Trinidad, in what he saw from the start as a vicarious and unrealized world, created questions and desires that could not be answered or satisfied by secondhand fictions. In an essay entitled 'Jasmine', which ends with his discovery that the scent and the name had both been known to him, but never put together, Naipaul explains the beginnings of his dissent or dissatisfaction:

> To us, without a mythology, all literatures were foreign. Trinidad was small, remote and unimportant, and we knew we could not hope to read in books of the life we saw about us. Books came from afar; they could offer only fantasy. . . . I went to books for fantasy; at the same time I required reality. (*OB*, pp. 24–5)

The questions posed by a colonial world are even more primal than the self-questioning of romanticism. Not so much questions like 'Who am I?', but rather – as Northrop Frye has phrased the most basic of them – 'Where is here?' Most conventional approaches toward literature's value for the young take the world for granted. What they take to be their task is the growth of some sense of a self, of a subjective reality, through the reading of literature. And since, by a virtuous circle we are not encouraged to look at too closely, our notions of the self and of subjectivity depend in great part on literary models, such approaches have until recently seemed sensible if not always successful. But what happens to the sense of literature if there is no cultural world, no shared and objective reality that the reader can start from and circle back to? Naipaul when young read books and stories, or had them read to him, as a way of peopling the void. He displaced to Port of Spain:

> the early parts of *The Mill on the Floss* . . . chapters of *Oliver Twist, Nicholas Nickleby, David Copperfield*; some of the novels of H. G. Wells; a short story by Conrad called "The Lagoon" . . . I never read to find out about foreign countries. Everything in books was foreign; everything had to be subjected to adaptation; and everything in, say, an English novel which worked and was of value to me at once ceased to be specifically English. (*OB*, p. 25)

Even Dickens, so often seen as the fairy godfather of Naipaul's early life and work, is subject to this creative misreading. So much of the picturesque and fantastic is either misread or rejected, 'All Dickens's descriptions of London', for example, and even the fiction that remains collapses into parable and fable, stories whose effect is not to excite the imagination but rather to console the spirit.

In a remarkable passage about the reading of Mr Biswas, this refusal of fiction is also shown to be the reconstruction of fiction into a strange kind of truth. Mr Biswas reads books about politics, but their presentation of misery and injustice leaves him feeling more desolate than ever:

> Then it was that he discovered the solace of Dickens. Without difficulty he transferred characters and settings to people and places he knew. In the grotesques of Dickens everything he feared and suffered from was ridiculed and diminished, so that his own anger, his own contempt became unnecessary, and he was given strength to bear with the most difficult part of his day: dressing in the morning, that daily affirmation of

faith in oneself, which at times was for him almost like an act of sacrifice. (*HMB*, p. 374)

This passage touches on Naipaul's own reading and writing in several ways, especially since *A House for Mr Biswas* springs as we shall see from his reading of his own father's stories. But it touches him to the quick and accounts for the dark origins of his own career as a writer by projecting on Mr Biswas the shame, contempt, and anguish that he resolved in himself through the grotesques and patois of his own early Trinidad fiction. Naipaul has repeatedly written of the 'great necessity' and 'panic' out of which he was driven to write, and has recently said of his wish to be a writer that it is 'mysterious . . . that this ambition should have come long before I could think of anything to write about' (*NYRB*, April 23, 1987, 7). This mysterious ambition would seem to have been his attempt to redeem in his own life his father's mostly thwarted hopes for a writer's career and the sufferings of his last years.

From what we have already seen, we can trace the hidden genealogy from father to son in Naipaul's Foreword to his father's stories, *The Adventures of Gurudeva*, which he had republished in England in 1976:

> The comedy was for others. My father remained unwilling to look at his own life. All that material, which might have committed him to longer work and a longer view, remained locked up and unused. Certain things can never become material. My father never in his life reached that point of rest from which he could look back at his past. His last years, when he found his voice as a writer, were years of especial distress and anxiety; he was part of the dereliction he wrote about. (*AG*, p. 18)

His father's death in 1953 made him feel not only grief but also a fear of extinction; his mother and sisters had become dependent on him, while he had remained a would-be writer living the lost life in London evoked in 'Tell Me Who to Kill'. And out of that fear of extinction, that confrontation with death, came the unlocking by the son of the father's material, of the comedy that 'was for others'. Naipaul has often pointed back to the liberation from fantasy and from the secondhand that was necessary for him to write the first two sentences of 'Bogart' and thereby become a writer. But there is also an allusive and filial relation between *A House for Mr Biswas*, the great unlocking of the father's material by the son, and the father's story 'They Named Him Mohun'.

*A House for Mr Biswas* is on several levels a fictive version of Naipaul's family history. The house desired by Mr Biswas is an object of desire created by the unhoused state of his own father, long homeless under the roof of his wife's extended family. The latter half of the novel turns around the relations of Mr Biswas and his son Anand, whose life and education parallel Naipaul's. Read as a whole, the novel redeems as it rewrites Anand's cold and self-centred replies to the letters his father wrote to him in England as his own life in Trinidad slid towards death. The first part of the son's novel begins,

> Shortly before he was born there had been another quarrel between Mr Biswas's mother Bipti and his father Raghu, and Bipti had taken her three children and walked all the way in the hot sun to the village where her mother Bissoondaye lived. (*HMB*, p. 15)

We might set this beside the opening of the father's story:

> Mohun's coming into this world of light was not an occasion of joy for anyone. There were reasons. In the first place, three months before his birth, Bipti, his mother, had left his father's home, as it turned out, never to return. With her two children – Sohani, aged four, and Krishna, a little over two years old – she had trudged seven miles to her mother's on a hot and dusty day. (*AG*, p. 125)

Far from concealing this link, Naipaul has dwelt upon its significance for him; and there can be no question of plagiarism when the second work so exceeds the first. Especially since the truth-telling and unlocking of material in *A House for Mr Biswas* is a deliberate revision – in more senses than one – of 'They Named Him Mohun'. It is also one more critique of fantasy and romance: 'My father hated his father for his cruelty

40

and meanness; yet when, in "They Named Him Mohun", he came to write about his father, he wrote a tale of pure romance, in which old ritual, lovingly described, can only lead to reconciliation. And my father, in spite of my encouragement, could never take the story any further' (*AG*, p. 16). This critical filiation, this 'great necessity' to rewrite and revive the father, was triggered by his death.

Thirty years later, hearing in Wiltshire on his return from Berlin that his younger sister was dying in Trinidad, he responds, 'since the death of my father in 1953, I had lived without grief. I took the news coldly, therefore; then I had hiccups; then I became concerned' (*EA*, p. 310). He returns to Trinidad in time for the Hindu rituals that follow her cremation, and it is the description of this ceremony that becomes the closing chapter of *The Enigma of Arrival*. That chapter closes with his double discovery that 'we remake the world for ourselves'. This last chapter then becomes a prologue to the book we have just read, because the ceremony of farewell for his sister forces him to face through her death the dreams that violate his sleep:

> It forced us to look on death. It forced me to face the death I had been contemplating at night, in my sleep; it fitted a real grief where melancholy had created a vacancy, as if to prepare me for the moment. It showed me life and man as the mystery, the true religion of men, the grief and the glory. And that was when, faced with a real death, and with this new wonder about men, I laid aside my drafts and hesitations and began to write very fast about Jack and his garden. (*EA*, p. 318)

A long and obsessive filiation and chain of words; necessary to account for Naipaul's fascination with fictions that are documents, documents that reveal the patterning of fiction, the pattern of something already written.

This filiation, which begins with a reading of Dickens as a way of withstanding the intimations of defeat and death in waking life, the intimation of preparing for sacrifice and death in the body's daily dressing in cloth that elsewhere is the

41

metaphor for a world undoing itself, and then that world itself; this chain of words that renews the father by rewriting his work and living the life denied to him, that renounces fantasy and romance in the name of stronger and truer evocations of the world – all of these are tied to death and finally unleashed by death. In the end, as Naipaul perceives 'life and man as the mystery, the true religion of men', he echoes the enlightened obsession of Michelet, who renounced romance and the novel in the name of his own truer history, which he then defined as the resurrection of the dead.

What Naipaul does not echo is the English novelistic tradition. We have seen how partial is his reading of even Dickens, and when he says what he does not like he tosses out most of what F. R. Leavis laid down as 'The Great Tradition': 'It would be easier to say what I don't like: Jane Austen, Hardy, Henry James, Conrad, and nearly every contemporary French novelist.'[6] Such a wholesale rejection of academic and avant-garde taste may have been a further token of his distaste at the way literature was reduced to texts at Oxford, where he spent four years reading English. And he did later change his mind about Conrad, though significantly more about the quality of his writings as meditations on the age than about their quality as fiction:

> My reservations about Conrad as a novelist remain. There is something flawed and unexercised about his creative imagination. . . . Conrad's value to me is that he is someone who sixty to seventy years ago meditated on my world, a world I recognize today. I feel this about no other writer of the century. His achievement derives from the honesty which is part of his difficulty, that 'scrupulous fidelity to the truth of my own sensation'. (*REP*, p. 210)

These last remarks are as much about himself as they are about Conrad; for those sensations, as Conrad complained in a letter to David Garnett, are all he has and they have with time faded away. As Naipaul observes, 'Its is the complaint of a writer who is missing a society, and is beginning to understand that fantasy or imagination can move more freely within a closed and ordered world' (*REP*, p. 217).

This freer movement or play of the imagination can be seen in Naipaul's only novel set in England among English characters, *Mr Stone and the Knights Companion*. The retiring Mr Stone is an anxious quietist whose fear of ageing and death, as they begin to intrude into his outlying part of London, drives him to devise a scheme for the retired of his company ('the Knights Companion') whose success still leaves him marooned in his own declining world. The novel plays not only with social and cultural codes but also with the whimsical and eccentric possibilities they create: the ageing librarian enticed into marriage even more slily than he entices a passing cat with a trail of cheese. Naipaul's mastery of an upholstered and yet vulnerable set of characters is flawless, and yet even this world undoes itself through a vision in Cornwall: 'Mr Stone never doubted that the incident could be rationally and simply explained. But that hallucinatory moment, when earth and life and senses had been suspended, remained with him. It was like an experience of nothingness, an experience of death' (*SKC*, p. 50). The absence or restriction of fantasy is otherwise the rule proved by this partial exception. Like his estrangement from novelistic realism, Naipaul's misgivings about fantasy are part of a larger attempt to transform the novel itself.

One of Wallace Stevens's *Adagia* offers the key to Naipaul, and beyond him to post-modernist writing: 'In the presence of extraordinary actuality, consciousness takes the place of imagination.'[7] Earlier in the century Joyce, Pound, and Eliot tried to throw the imagination like a great tent or marquee over the upheavals and auctions of their time, Dublin was to be reimagined as the *Odyssey*, both the Englightenment and the alphabet were to be written out of the *Encyclopedia* and the result called the *Cantos*, even Eliot tried to do the *Waste Land* (and the police) in different voices before those voices were shot to pieces by the shorter pencil of Pound. The result of this attempt to imagine everything was at times the immense exhaustion of the encyclopedic work, at other times the vengeful return of the romantic fragment. The word 'experimental' seemed to be welded to the word 'style'.

The consequences of this for the novel were curious, and they were once brought home to me by Claude Simon's comments about his *La Route des Flandres* (*The Flanders Road*), a great book and one that is usually thought to embody the experimental ambition of the *nouveau roman*. No, said Simon to his Zurich audience, I wrote it that way because that is how I experienced it. 'It' was the shattering defeat of France in 1940, and Simon's experience of this was as a cavalry trooper in a regiment that in the course of the campaign, which is also the course of the book, was virtually annihilated. What he was aiming at was not an experiment but an experience that subverted every accepted way of expressing it. Simon's rich and sensuous prose is as much a counter-balance to the shock of *Blitzkrieg* as Naipaul's antiseptic irony is to the defilement and disorder that undoes the world he knows. Both are presented to the reader as the discourse of consciousness rather than as a feat of the imagination.

In writing about his intentions in *The Enigma of Arrival*, which transforms the novel into a meditation and a *mémoire intérieure*, he uses almost the same words as Simon:

> I have just finished a book in which at last, as I think, I have managed to integrate this business of reinterpreting with my narrative.
>
> My aim was truth, truth to a particular experience, containing a definition of the writing self. (*NYRB*, 23 April 1987, 7)

Literary theory, notably what passes under the name of deconstruction, has in recent years drawn our attention to the unstable relations between style and subject, between rhetoric and reference, in any piece of writing. Stress has been laid on the need to unmask the rhetorical figures that hide behind the work's apparent reference to a world outside itself, to reveal the workings of the style that does so much to create its subject. Subject here can mean the self as well as the material out of which the narrative is made, and this way of reading has been a necessary response to works like Rousseau's *Confessions* and Wordsworth's *Prelude*, where the subject as story is revealed to be the subject as the writing self. This can hardly be a revelation about a writer such as Naipaul, who tells us that he writes to find out who he is, and who says in so many words that the experience he aims to be faithful to has at its centre 'a definition of the writing self'. It could be objected that Naipaul too makes up the apparently solid prior experience out of shadowy and belated metaphors. How much of an objection is this, though, to a writer who asserts the ungraspable evanescence of his subject and tropes the world as unravelling cloth? What Naipaul has illumined in his writing is the other side or converse of this unstable relation between rhetoric and reference, the back-spin by which the enigma or anguish of a narrative's subject deflects or distorts the rhetorical patterns that project that subject. We will deal with this at greater length before long, but for now an example from *A Bend in the River* may suggest what this means.

This novel, as we have seen, revisits *Heart of Darkness* to tell a story that is even more unnerving than Conrad's. There may have been a hint to Naipaul in Marlow's opening words about the darkness that England once was and the aboriginal world of the Romans in Britain: 'Here and there a military camp lost in a wilderness, like a needle in a bundle of hay – cold, fog, tempests, disease, exile, and death – death skulking in the air, in the water, in the bush' (pp. 30–1). Naipaul may not have needed this hint because, as we shall see, he had already become fascinated by ancient narratives and modern reinterpretations of the rise and corruption of the Roman Republic, the decline and fall of the Empire. His fascination was not remote or impersonal, and led first to his travels to Africa, then to the document entitled 'A New King for the Congo: Mobutu and the Nihilism of Africa', first published in 1975, *REP*. All of these texts and pretexts run through the narrative of Salim, who carries within himself, upriver and inland from the east coast of Africa, a history as murky and remote as Naipaul's. This likeness may be more than glancing, as Salim's remarks about his ancestry and family history suggest. Although

Muslim, he and his family feel closer to the Hindus of north-western India who are their distant ancestors. Their story is the story of displacement and upheaval that Naipaul's family knew in Trinidad, but here the story has been transferred to the shores of the Indian Ocean.

By the time the novel appeared four years later, this subject and its enigma, its underlying mystery and *aporia*, has expanded outward to include the entire erased history of the Congo – African kingdoms, Arab trading empire, Belgian colony, and now under Mobutu the kingdom of Zaire – during a period that foretells yet another violent erasure. It has expanded inward to embody this erasure in characters – African, Arab, Belgian – who by their words and acts insist on the need to 'trample on the past'. Their only alternative is to dwell on a destroyed past. Forgetting the past does not confer the vitality promised by Nietzsche. It merely ensures the elimination in its turn of the present created by the destruction of memory.

As the narrator Salim tries to understand his feeling that some blank or omission or dishonesty separates him from Indar, who like him has fled from the end of another world on the east coast of Africa, he concludes:

> That omission was our own past, the smashed life of our community. Indar had referred to that at our first meeting that morning in the shop. He said that he had learned to trample on the past. In the beginning it had been like trampling on a garden; later it had become like walking on ground. (*ABR*, p. 131)

This omission or dishonesty not only comes to twist the metaphorical and psychological shape of the characters, but questions the significance of the story that involves and undoes them. The Belgian Raymond, who has stayed on to become the ruler's court historian, has been reading many of the books that fascinate Naipaul; and they have given him misgivings about the story as well as the history he is supposed to write:

> I don't think it is sufficiently understood how hard it is to

46

write about what has never been written about before. The occasional academic paper on a particular subject, the Bapende rebellion or whatever – that has its own form. The larger narrative is another matter. That's why I have begun to consider Theodor Mommsen the giant of modern historical writing. . . . Of course Theodor Mommsen had the comfort of knowing that his subject was a great one. Those of us who work in our particular field have no such assurance. We have no idea of the value posterity will place on the events we attempt to chronicle. We have no idea where the contingent is going. We can only carry on. (*ABR*, p.143)

These are characters leading what Adorno would call damaged lives; but even more, they are interpreters whose limits call into question the story they are telling.

Both Indar and Raymond also evoke aspects of Naipaul that elsewhere appear in the documents that underlie his novels. Indar's simile that changes from 'trampling on a garden' to 'walking on ground', for example, may be one of the seeds that caused the obsessive growth in Naipaul's imagination of what was to become Jack's garden, which was later to become the starting-point for *The Enigma of Arrival*. This garden matters to Naipaul not only because Jack tended it so well, but also because after his death, dying with the freezing lungs that later threaten Naipaul, his garden is neglected and 'trampled on', like several other gardens on what is a large and neglected estate. And just as 'trampling on a garden' becomes a simile for violation of the past, 'walking on ground' becomes Naipaul's description of natural behaviour and self-renewal after his arrival in Wiltshire. Even more plainly, Raymond's enthusiasm for Roman history, and for the 'troubled years of the later Republic', echo Naipaul's account of his interests and reading pleasures:

Though I am impressed by the grandeur and lastingness of the imperial achievement, like Suetonius and Tacitus as much as anyone, my special interest is the last century of the Republic, when Rome seems to come out of legend into 'modern' times. The great figures of this period, perhaps

because of chauvinistic commentators, seem straightfor-
ward and contemporary; but they are always, finally, elus-
ive. I cannot understand Cicero; Pompey is a mystery. The
more I read the more I see that there are corners of the
Roman mind I can never enter. This is their fascination.
(*The Times*, 13 July 1961, 13)

Twenty-five years later, the mystery of the Republic and
Naipaul's desire to enter into it, the subject and history that had
enticed him with their elusiveness, were to unsettle and enrich
another metaphor that became the dominant image of *The
Enigma of Arrival*.

This is Naipaul's reinterpretation of de Chirico's painting of
the same title: 'My story was to be set in classical times, in the
Mediterranean. My narrator would write plainly, without any
attempt at period style or historical explanation of his period'
(*EA*, p. 92). There can be little doubt about the referential
subject here, as Naipaul goes on to describe something that
sounds rather like Broch's *Death of Virgil*. The appeal of this
subject is all the greater because it is such an apparent contrast
to the story he is then bogged down in. This is the novella 'In a
Free State', which comes to be reimagined (or is it disfigured?)
by the writer's meditations on the Wiltshire valley outside his
cottage window and on the story that interprets de Chirico, the
story he is *not* writing:

> The idea of living in my imagination in that classical
> Roman world was attractive to me. A beautiful, clear,
> dangerous world, far removed from the setting in which I
> had found myself; the story, more a mood than a story,
> so different from the book on which I was working. (*EA*,
> pp. 92–3)

The ending of that other story, set in Africa, may at first seem to
have nothing to do with the Roman world or with de Chirico's
picture. But as Naipaul comes to see, the expatriate English-
man Bobby, who at story's end has been humiliated and beaten
by the drunken soldiery in a tribal war, saving himself inside
the gates of the European compound and yet, perhaps, losing
what remained of his life in Africa – this figure may be another

version of the narrator and protagonist of the enigmatic story set in the Roman world. Realizing that he is lost, he tries to escape back to his ship, but cannot find his way to the port and comes close to being killed:

> I imagined some religious ritual in which, led on by kindly people, he would unwittingly take part and find himself back on the quayside of arrival. He has been saved; the world is as he remembered it. Only one thing is missing now. Above the cut-out walls and buildings there is no mast, no sail. The antique ship has gone. The traveller has lived out his life. (*EA* p. 92)

Although this reverie is in turn linked to a dream in which he witnesses his own death, Naipaul seems to be both maker and victim of an interlinked story that is actually one story; and that story, to be told, requires the enigma of the Roman world and its breakdown, the enigma of arrival and death.

We might close this account of Naipaul's undoing of fiction and fantasy by recalling what he *does* read and reflect on in his own work. In praising Conrad, he took pains to say that he had done what the novel no longer seemed to do, shown us a world that is 'always new'. This long withdrawal of the novel, that was once so 'obtrusive', follows in his eyes from the weakening of the societies that provoked the realistic fiction of the past. The inward turn of the narrative has accompanied an inward turn in the myth of the writer. Hence,

> The novel as a form no longer carries conviction. Experimentation, not aimed at the real difficulties, has corrupted response; and there is great confusion in the minds of readers and writers about the purpose of the novel. . . . And so the world we inhabit, which is always new, goes by unexamined, made ordinary by the camera, unmeditated on; and there is no one to awaken the sense of wonder. (*REP*, pp. 217–18)

The camera's part in making the world banal is deftly put, and this remark shows how close Naipaul is to Stevens's notion of extraordinary reality. And if we were to ask ourselves what

49

kinds of narrative correspond to the response of consciousness to a world 'always new' – books of travel, of natural observation, histories of great crises – we discover that Naipaul was steeped in them, and that they in turn pervade his work. Raymond's complaint that people do not grasp 'how hard it is to write about what has never been written about before' points to a central problem, as Ronald Paulson has shown in considering visual as well as verbal responses to the French Revolution.[8] Just as attempts to portray revolutionary martyrs, such as David's *Death of Marat*, are driven back to Pietàs out of the past, so Raymond (and Naipaul) are driven back to Mommsen (and Gibbon) in an attempt to interpret the 'extraordinary actuality' of political and psychological convulsions in the modern world.

Naipaul's boldest discovery is that historical cycles, whose fullest turning appears in contemporary and later interpretations of Roman history, can be reinterpreted through narratives that expose not only the outward actuality of disorder, through 'images of revolt and flying off', but also the inward and extraordinary actuality of lostness and rage expressed by primitives and decadents, by those who have been cast up or cast away by history. This counterpoising of two kinds of narrative accounts for the unusual structure of *In a Free State*. The opening and closing journal entries present from without, observed by the writer as a recorder of his times, the abandonment expressed from within, from out of the depths, by the narrators of the two stories. After this speaking in barbarian tongues, the author, implied and actual, of the journal entries returns in the title-novella to interpret a journey into fear made new and fresh by the reversion to savagery of guardians and servants: ravening dogs, murderous servants, mutinous troops. A story, as we have seen, retold in the menacing Mediterranean world of ancient Rome. This interplay between the fictional, the historical, and the ethnographic; between the cycle and the psyche, accounts for the haunting and to some readers enigmatic ending of *In a Free State*. The journal writer meets again in Egypt, among the tombs and palaces of Luxor, the Chinese circus he had met earlier in Milan. Circus and cycle, the encounter of empires, meeting and meeting again; and as the Chinese leave they once again present gifts to their waiters, medals and postcards of peonies:

> Peonies, China! So many empires had come here. Not far from where we were was the colossus on whose shin the Emperor Hadrian had caused to be carved verses in praise of himself, to commemorate his visit. On the other bank, not far from the Winter Palace, was a stone with a rougher Roman inscription marking the southern limit of the Empire, defining an area of retreat. Now another, more remote empire was announcing itself. A medal, a postcard; and all that was asked in return was anger and a sense of injustice. (*IFS*, pp. 245–6)

These reflections owe something to the ironic style of Gibbon, the sense of fate we find in Spengler. But they modulate into the sense of wonder before a new and inviolate land that Naipaul found in Sir Walter Ralegh's visions of El Dorado, and that in its turn becomes the narrative of a vanishing dream, the enabling fiction of modern ethnography. In a magnificent sentence, Naipaul sees it as fictive and fateful, as an image of desire: 'Perhaps that vision of the land, in which the Nile was only water, a blue-green chevron, had always been a fabrication, a cause for yearning, something for the tomb' (*IFS*, p. 246). This double insight into history and sorcery Naipaul found in Fustel de Coulanges, who dreamed the anthropologist's dream within the archival world of Roman history, and in Jacques Soustelle, who transferred the romance of defeat from ancient Mexico to Gaullist France, from metaphor to murder.[9] This insight accounts in part for the power of the book's last paragraph:

> The air-conditioning in the coach didn't work well; but that may have been because the two Negro attendants, still with the habits of the village, preferred to sit before the open doors to chat. Sand and dust blew in all day; it was hot until the sun set and everything went black against the red sky. In the dimly lit waiting-room of Cairo station there were more sprawled soldiers from Sinai, peasants in bulky woollen

51

uniforms going back on leave to their villages. Seventeen
months later these men, or men like them, were to know total
defeat in the desert; and news photographs taken from
helicopters flying down low were to show them lost, trying
to walk back home, casting long shadows on the sand. (*IFS*,
p. 246)

Some of these details are reported by a narrator who has read
and written many a travel book: the ineffectual air-
conditioning, the blowing sand and red sky, even the soldiers in
the train station. But the rising cadences of the prose, and the
anthropologist's note in 'still with the habits of the village',
draw the reader upward and onward toward that vision at the
end. This is a vision of an end to come that is historical as well
as prophetic, like the moment in the *Reflections on the French
Revolution* when Burke writes, 'History will record . . .'. Like
that moment, it is a vision that has to confront the world, to
recognize in these lost soldiers images from the Six Days' War,
the Egyptian army's collapse before the Israeli attacks in the
Sinai Desert. There may also be an echo, a self-allusion, to the
lost and almost sacrificed traveller in Naipaul's unwritten story
about de Chirico's painting. It was this story, we recall, that
repeated the African story of the expatriates' attempt to get
back home through another war, after another empire, after
other defeats. Naipaul's power to translate between history
and fiction, between the traveller's dream and the ethnographer's romance, which obsessively marks and distinguishes his
work, is a power that Claude Lévi-Strauss has defined as the
power to make myths. And that, as we shall see, was from the
start a strength and a need in Naipaul's life and work.

# 3

# ISLANDS IN AIR

That a Man may be scarce less ignorant of his own powers, than an Oyster of its pearl, or a Rock of its diamond; that he may possess dormant, unsuspected abilities . . . is evident from the sudden eruption of some men, out of perfect obscurity, into publick admiration . . . not more to the world's great surprize, than their own. Few authors of distinction but have experienced something of this nature, at the first beamings of their yet unsuspected Genius on their hitherto dark Composition: The writer starts at it, as at a lucid Meteor in the night; is much surprized; can scarce believe it true. During his happy confusion, it may be said to him, as to Eve at the Lake,
*What there thou seest, fair creature! is thyself.* (Edward Young, *Conjectures on Original Composition*)

V. S. Naipaul once identified his interests in life and literature – the past, countries strange or big, long trips 'in exciting weather' – as contrast to the Trinidad of his birth and upbringing. There, he observed, on 'a very small, unimportant island, where no building was 150 years old, and where the weather never varied', was born his desire to leave and go somewhere altogether elsewhere.[10] We have seen how his beginnings as a writer, his creative point of departure, came through a double return to the West Indies. There was first his return through memory to 'Bogart' and the language of the tribe, then his return through allusion and revision to his father's stories and the second beginning of *A House for Mr Biswas*. In his Foreword to the publication of these stories in England, however, Naipaul spoke for both his father and himself when he said, quoting Derek Walcott's shared self-description, *We, being all islands in air,* 'The writer begins with his talent, finds confidence in his talent, but then discovers that it isn't enough, that, in a society as deformed as ours, by the exercise of his talent he has set himself adrift' (*AG*, p. 22). Putting aside for the moment the judgement on the Caribbean world implied by this double bind, we can still notice that much of Naipaul's early writing was an attempt to overcome or escape it by re-forming that society through his own work.

His first attempt was *The Middle Passage*, which seeks to locate and characterize, to give a local habitation and a name, to the various parts of the colonial rim of South America and the string of islands, Windward and Leeward, stretching up toward Puerto Rico. Naipaul's travels covered a good part of the Spanish Main, a term whose double meaning and change of meaning is a thumbnail sketch of the region's history. It first meant the northern coast of South America, where the Spanish Empire was early settled and extended by priests, conquistadors, and seekers after El Dorado; it was the 'Spanish Mainland'. As the focus of European interest shifted toward sugar, cocoa, and coffee, the name too shifted, to the waters of the Caribbean, the 'North Sea' dominated by the islands and lands of the Viceroyalty of New Spain; it had become the 'Main Spanish Sea'. Growing and gathering these crops in the heat and fever of the islands was work white men could not or would not do, and over the years millions of slaves were brought over from Africa on the second leg of a triangular route that ran from English ports, especially Liverpool and Bristol, to West Africa, then on to the West Indies and the southern American States. Finally, carrying what changed from luxuries into everyday goods over three centuries, the ships returned to England. Hence the book's title and a hint of what drove Naipaul to choose it.

After so much slave labour and so many years, virtually nothing created or creative had been left behind. Even the memory of their origins was erased: 'Twenty million Africans made the middle passage, and scarcely an African name remains in the New World. Until the other day African tribesmen on the screen excited derisive West Indian laughter' (*MP*, p. 72). Even here Naipaul identifies the tasks and powers of

54

novelists, poets, and historians to create memories and myths without which a culture could not exist, and did not; the fault in his eyes of West Indian writers. He has not been forgiven for writing what many of his contemporaries read as a fault-finding tour. And yet a later reading of *The Middle Passage*, *The Loss of El Dorado*, and *The Mimic Men* shows that he was painfully attempting what many South American writers have been engaged in over the past generation: the discovery of myth and the recovery of memory.

Naipaul has come over time to recognize what a doubtful and even dubious enterprise this can be. Doubtful, because the West Indies, even more than other parts of the New World, lack the ruins out of which the western imagination has reconstructed monuments and memories. Gibbon, who recognized the erosive vandalism of time and war, none the less assumed that his history of decline and fall could be written backwards out of his musings among the ruins of the Capitol which, though more fragile than the Pyramids, still remained; for 'The art of man is able to construct monuments far more permanent than the narrow span of his own existence.'[11] It could even be said that these reconstructed ruins dominate all the documents used by Gibbon, giving to history that pervasive irony, not of Ozymandias or Ecclesiastes, but rather of a pagan satirist, dispossessed and contemptuous of 'the barefoot friars . . . singing vespers in the Temple of Jupiter'. To be barefoot or shoeless in the West Indies, as Naipaul early observed, was a mark of shame rather than a badge of romantic achievement. Monuments of wood in a region whose economy often seemed to be based on a policy compressed in the phrase 'insuranburn', and whose favoured building material seemed to be corrugated iron, had left few ruins behind to muse among. The murder and mass suicides of the aboriginal Carib Indians had taken that primordial memory into the void, into trampled graves or into the sea beating against the cliffs from which they had jumped. And so it seemed to have gone ever since, a fragile and tainted fantasy, the road to slave poisonings and their modern reversal among the fanatics of Jonestown.

After the erasure of the Indians came the longer oppression

of the African slaves on the plantations, and the abolitions of slavery created the indenture system that brought hundreds of thousands of East Indians to the West Indies, still to cut the sugarcane that has always been the cruellest of crops, the ugliest kind of farming; featureless fields and a harvest among burnt-over stalks and leaves, so that even the sugarcane itself seems to testify to the dereliction it has caused. And that is the word and condition as Naipaul saw it repeated on his travels. On leaving Surinam, for example, he left 'A derelict man in a derelict land; a man discovering himself, with surprise and resignation, lost in a landscape which had never ceased to be unreal because the scene of an enforced and always temporary residence' (*MP*, p. 209). The man was an Indian, like Naipaul's ancestors, one of those who had made the longest voyage, and who left with the writer a sense of 'the full desolation that came to those who made the middle passage'.

This vision of the West Indies is very different from the tourist-poster paradise that is a marginal note in Naipaul's books; but it also may seem to exclude both the untidy energy of his early stories and the obsessive reveries of *The Loss of El Dorado*. The marginalizing of tourism could be taken as accuracy on his part. Trinidad has never had, apart from Carnival, much appeal to tourists: only the North coast looks like the posters, and the currents there make swimming risky. The coming of the Americans that matters in the early stories is the wartime coming of the military, the building of the bases that signified both a new wealth and an end to an older Empire:

Then the war came. Hitler invaded France and the Americans invaded Trinidad. Lord Invader made a hit with his calypso:
    I was living with my decent and contented wife
    Until the soldiers came and broke up my life.

For the first time in Trinidad there was work for everybody, and the Americans paid well. Invader sang:

Father, mother, and daughter
Working for the Yankee dollar!
Money in the land!
The Yankee dollar, oh!

Edward stopped working in the cow-pen and got a job with the Americans at Chaguaramas.

Hat said, 'Edward, I think you foolish to do that. The Americans ain't here forever and ever. It ain't have no sense in going off and working for big money and then not having nothing to eat after three four years.'

Edward said, 'This war looks as though it go last a long time. And the Americans not like the British, you know. They does make you work hard, but they does pay for it.' (*MS*, p. 143–4)

The playing off of history, calypso, and fiction, are all part of the comic fantasy of the early stories. But as Naipaul's vision of the Caribbean past grows through his unearthing and bringing to light of documents that showed the clandestine fantasy of slave society, he realizes that so much of the calypso satire and costuming at Carnival resonate out of that past silence:

It is the silence of all serfdom. . . . The poisonings, a love-potion given to a woman with hands calloused from labour, a wise old sorcerer, the obeah, the drumming and the jumping-up at every opportunity: this is what comes to the surface. It suggests a whole underground life of fantasy, linking creole Negroes, French Negroes and English Negroes.

The New World as make-believe: this Negro fantasy life changed and developed. In Trinidad, an immigrant island, it had become many-featured, a dream beyond labour and more real than labour, of power and prettiness, of titles, flags and uniforms, kings and queens and courtiers. The planter, looking at his Negroes and seeing only Negroes, never knew . . . the planter didn't know that that Negro carter, an especially stupid Negro, was a king at night, with twelve courtiers and a uniform of his own: a black coat with a scarlet collar and a green ribbon over one shoulder, a hat with a black cockade. (*LED*, pp. 291–2)

This passage shows the beginnings of what later became the signature and the spoor of Naipaul's writing; his insistence on the need to translate the festive or obscure details of his West Indian world into the larger significance of history and myth. The principle of perception that underlies this drive to translate and transform is most clearly expressed in a remark he made about India, about the world out of which his own life in Trinidad came to him as a partial translation.

The India he speaks of is the India of Kipling; even more locally, it is the Simla of the Raj, the hill town and fairyland that Kipling made part of an English vernacular. Naipaul recognizes in Simla, for all its decay, the streets and houses and shops of Kipling's stories and observes, 'No city or landscape is truly real unless it has been given the quantity of myth by writer, painter or by its association with great events' (*AD*, p. 194). What seems most to have disturbed Naipaul about Trinidad and the Caribbean, what drove him away toward England, was this unreality, this result of an absence of myth. After comparing his return to the West Indies on a Spanish immigrant ship to the earlier voyages of the slave ships on the middle passage, he brings his description to an end:

> It would go from St Kitts to Grenada to Trinidad to Barbados: one journey answering another: the climax and futility of the West Indian adventure . . . no civilization as in Spanish America, no great revolution as in Haiti or the American colonies. There were only plantations, prosperity, decline, neglect: the size of the islands called for nothing else. (*MP*, p. 27)

Even though it advances through a series of denials, this description is a first step toward significance: the second voyage becomes a translation of the first. The paradox or absurdity of this, which is later repeated in the grasping of illusion at the end of *An Area of Darkness*, is that significance arises out of the assertion of insignificance: something comes of nothing.

It may be that this paradox hides a deep truth about myth, which seems always to translate the unknown or unknowable into metaphors or stories we can recognize or follow. How this mythic manner of translation works has been described by Claude Lévi-Strauss, who has also proposed the theory that myth consists of translations and comparisons:

> Every myth poses a problem and deals with it by showing that it is analogous with other problems; or again myth may deal simultaneously with several problems by showing that they are analogues of one another. . . . To oversimplify, we could say that myth is a system of logical operations defined by the method of 'it's when' or 'it's like'. . . . Mythic thinking thus has the original quality of working between several codes. Each takes from one domain of experience the latent properties that allow comparisons with other domains, in a word, *to translate* one into another; just as a text may be barely intelligible in only one language will, if it is rendered into several, perhaps let shine out from these different versions a richer and deeper sense than any of them, partial and mutilated, could allow access to if each version were to be taken separately.[12]

This is how, to oversimplify in turn, Naipaul translates the partial and mutilated records and stories of the West Indies into other languages; into the discourse of empire and utopia, the language of travel and discovery. As he finds himself faced by increasingly obscure or superstitious narratives, in India or the world of Islam, he translates what he sees and hears into the codes of the anthropologist, whose hard task it is to translate what the historian would consider superstition into an account that will convey and preserve the superstitious and miraculous without seeming to believe in it, without being tainted by its irrationality. This task, together with his Brahmin dread of pollution, accounts for the contrastive translations in both his fictional and non-fictional books. What is squalid or pidgin is translated through and into a language that is refined and immaculate.

The denser the cloud of unknowing around a character or fantasy, the more radiant his analogues and metaphors, his *réflexion mythique*. This way of reflecting and translating often leaves an impression of mockery and satire, echoes of Hume writing about miracles or Gibbon about barefoot friars – or even Evelyn Waugh writing in *Black Mischief* about barefoot soldiers who stay that way by eating the boots issued to make them look more part of the modern world. And yet he has also shown how the process of working between codes can go in several directions. Just as he had as a child in Trinidad projected fantasies derived from English literature on to the countryside and people around him, so too, back in England and writing *In a Free State*, he observes in *The Enigma of Arrival*:

> Now, in Wiltshire in winter, a writer now rather than a reader, I worked the child's fantasy the other way. I projected the solitude and emptiness and menace of my Africa on to the land around me. And when four days later the fog lifted and I went walking, something of the Africa of my story adhered to the land I saw. (*EA*, p. 155)

There seems to be a reciprocal or seesaw relation between these codes; between solitude and teeming life, emptiness and fullness, purity and pollution. The last pairing would not surprise an anthropologist, for whom any attempt to deal with either pollution or purity, which are related even in their etymology, seems to provoke ritual and discourse about the other.[13]

What the conquistadors and their English rivals were searching for in *The Loss of El Dorado*, whose title is such a pairing, was not just gold, but

> the complete unviolated world. Such a world had existed and the Spaniards wished to have the adventure again. The story grew subtler with Spanish failure. It took the Spaniards beyond the realities of their life in the bush; it teased every deprived sense. (*LED*, p. 31)

The insight of this passage goes beyond its subject. Its pairing of a sense of loss and a quickening of the imagination, of absence that provokes ever more subtle narratives of presence, hints at what quickens Naipaul's imagination. It also unveils a far-reaching paradox about writing that has been articulated in the critical theory of Jacques Derrida – the more fully writing 'teases every deprived sense' with the stories and rhetoric of presence, the more nakedly it reveals itself to be about absence. In a magnificent drowning of the reader's senses that amplifies through Ralegh's narrative his own reflections on the fleeting possession of El Dorado, Naipaul shows how far this translation of opposites and enigmas can go:

> To be received among them as a liberator: that was part of the dream. In Ralegh's memory those six days of Indian welcome on the Orinoco blended with the memory of a magical forest, of a 'mountaine of cristall' seen from a distance, 'like a white church-tower of an exceeding height', over which a mighty river poured, touching no part of the mountain. To this there was added the knowledge of a 'mine', never seen. In the end it drew him out of the Tower of London, which was his perfect setting, perhaps subconsciously sought, where, liberated from his inadequacy in the role the age imposed on him, he reached that stillness where the fact of life and action was reconciled with the fact of death. This was what he had plundered, this latecoming to the quest that destroyed so many. (*LED*, p. 69)

The narrator doubles his narrative through Ralegh's account, provoked by the mirage of El Dorado into repeating his images and similes. Naipaul also doubles himself in the figure of Ralegh in the Tower, in the figure of the narrator as a prisoner or exile, one who needs his estrangement and stillness if he is to recover through the narrative of memory the experience of vision he once had by glimpses and now has no longer. These two ways of telling a story – doubling an absent narrator – could be taken as descriptions or even as allegories of two other novels whose setting is the West Indies. These are *A House for Mr Biswas* and *The Mimic Men*; and it is to them, by way of *The Enigma of Arrival*, that we shall now turn and return.

After writing *The Loss of El Dorado* and sending it off to an American publisher, who was expecting something more like a guide to Port of Spain for a series on cities, Naipaul pulled up stakes in England and set off on a voyage that took him first to the region he had just created in his book: 'the journey might have been planned by a man wishing to move backwards in time, to see his history take concrete expression' (*EA*, p. 149). Writing his visionary book and creating a history out of neglected documents had given him a second historical relation with his origins that coexisted with the fictive relation created by his novels:

> I had given myself a past, and a romance of the past. One of the loose ends in my mind had vanished; a little chasm filled. And though something like Haitian anarchy seemed to threaten my little island, and though physically I no longer belonged to the place, yet the romance by which I had attached it to the rest of the world continued to be possessed by me as much as the imaginative worlds of my other, fictional books. (*EA*, pp. 149–50)

He had conferred an identity and a sense of place on himself, a habitation and a name, through the books he had written. Novels and history alike had gone to create a 'romance' that could only survive through the illusion of realism, the illusion that nothing has been omitted from a fiction that can and must be accepted as an alternative world. This is the illusion conferred by the realistic novel of the nineteenth century, by *Madame Bovary* or *Middlemarch*; and this too is the illusion conferred by *A House for Mr Biswas*. There are still some readers who accept such fictions as alternatives or representations, who do not grasp how much of their power lies in the desire or the need to displace and destroy the world outside themselves. Since Naipaul's development as a writer depends upon his recognition that realism, both fictional and historical, is illusory, we should look more closely into and beyond *A House for Mr Biswas* to see what might underlie and undermine its realism.

If the illusion of realism depends upon apparent completeness and unforced unnaturalness, that of modernism depends on omission, fragmentation, and self-conscious artifice. And yet we notice in reading even *Middlemarch*, generally taken as a standard of realism, how much it is entangled in nostalgia, romance, and even the kind of coincidence that Bulstrode brings into the novel. Joyce's *Ulysses* attempts and claims a total reconstruction of Dublin as it was on the 16 June 1904, a claim that is again tied to the attempt made by nineteenth-century historians like Ranke to recount a world and a time 'wie es eigentlich war', the way it really was. And yet, as Stanislaus Joyce wrote to his brother after reading *Ulysses*, 'Where so much has been recorded, I object to what has been omitted.'[14] Ranke's claim is usually thought to rest on the adverb *eigentlich* or *really*, a claim to be made good through archival zeal and narrative skill. But the claim rests much more shakily on *es* and *war*, on our unexamined assumptions about *it*, about the selection and fabrication necessary to create an event or period, and about *was*, about the imaginative leap needed to bring the past into our present.

The initial claims made by the narrator in *A House for Mr Biswas* are all the bolder for being so relaxed. They are the claims to our attention made by an omniscient author modestly disguised as a story-teller. Even more modestly, as a story-teller who shows his artless candour by papering over the holes in his narrative with ages, dates, debts and dimensions: 'Mr Biswas was forty-six, and had four children. He had no money. His wife Shama had no money. On the house on Sikkim Street Mr Biswas owed, and had been owing for four years, three thousands dollars' (*HMB*, p. 7). As the narrative continues we begin to notice that the implied author who jogs the memory (or is it the wrist?) of our story-teller betrays signs of a subtle literary sense and a feeling of kinship with Mr Biswas as a writer, as someone whose life will also be recorded (or is it fantasized?) in his own work. Here is how he recounts the backhanded welcome Mr Biswas receives from his mother Bipti when he returns to a house that is not a home for either of them:

> He did not see at the time how absurd and touching her behaviour was: welcoming him back to a hut that didn't belong to her, giving him food that wasn't hers. But the memory remained, and nearly thirty years later, when he was a member of a small literary group in Port of Spain, he wrote and read out a simple poem in blank verse about this

63

meeting. The disappointment, his surliness, all the un-
pleasantness was ignored, and the circumstances improved
to allegory: the journey, the welcome, the food, the shelter.
(*HMB*, p. 57)

We have already seen that in retelling the story of Mohun, the
story his father had already begun years before, Naipaul is
doubling both an absent narrative and an absent narrator. The
presence of this doubling, like that of a wrinkled sheet under
one laid flat, far from having the effect of completeness,
reminds us that there is something hidden underneath, that the
wholeness of this novel is paradoxically lessened by its insistence on telling us more. But its interest as a commingling of
stories, some told, some suppressed, is increased by these hints
of self-awareness. There is a warning sign at French railway
crossings that says, when translated, 'One train can hide
another', and this warning can be further translated and used
against attempts to take either Naipaul or realism at face value.
But it can be translated yet again into a sign of his genius for
doubling narratives, both in the ways we have seen and in
making them analogues of historical visions that we see by
glimpses on the margins of the novel's pages.

A final example might serve to show how intimately and
incipiently the novel anticipates the designs and compulsions
of *The Loss of El Dorado*. Early in his childhood, Mr Biswas's
mother sells off land that was also his birthplace:

the land Bipti had sold so cheaply to Dhari was later found to
be rich with oil. And when Mr Biswas was working on a
feature article for the magazine section of the *Sunday Sen-
tinel* – RALEIGH'S DREAM COMES TRUE, said the headline, 'But the Gold is Black. Only the Earth is Yellow. Only
the Bush Green' (*HMB*, p. 41)

The consequence of this parodic discovery of El Dorado is that
Mr Biswas loses all contact with his past, which is trampled
into the mire:

when Mr Biswas looked for the place where he had spent his
early years he saw nothing but oil derricks and grimy pumps,

64

see-sawing, see-sawing, endlessly, surrounded by red No Smoking notices. His grandparents' house had also disappeared, and when huts of mud and grass are pulled down they leave no trace. His navel-string, buried on that inauspicious night, and his sixth finger, buried not long after, had turned to dust. . . . The stream where he had watched the black fish had been dammed, diverted into a reservoir, and its winding, irregular bed covered by straight lawns, streets and drives. The world carried no witness to Mr Biswas's birth and early years. (*HMB*, p. 41)

It is this erasure of the past that Naipaul later assigns to himself and makes his reason for writing the later book about Ralegh, Picton, and the lost history of Trinidad. On one level the result is personal, 'I had given myself a past, and a romance of the past'. On another it is historical, though still expressed in personal terms:

Port of Spain was a place where things had happened and nothing showed. Only people remained, and their past had dropped out of all the history books. Picton was the name of a street; no one knew more. History was a fairy-tale about Columbus and a fairy-tale about the strange customs of the Aboriginal Caribs and Arawaks; it was impossible now to set them in a landscape. (*LED*, p. 375)

Some placings are more impossible than others, and both the title and name of *The Loss of El Dorado* had already been placed in *A House for Mr Biswas* and a story it doubles and repeats. The headline and subtitles of the article Mr Biswas wrote about the oil-field that dispossessed him alludes to and in part quotes from a story written by Naipaul's father about the dispossessed in another such place. This story, 'In the Village', says of its setting, 'in this village all that looked yellow was mostly dirt, and all that looked green was mostly bush'. But that is not all: the village in the story is called El Dorado, and outside the story El Dorado was the village in Trinidad where Naipaul's father grew up and where 'the wish to be a writer' came to him (*AG*, p. 12).

So many tracks and traces lead into and out of *The Loss of El Dorado*. While Naipaul was revisiting the history he had created in that book by travelling around the Caribbean; or rather, while he was trying to read through and past the palimpsest of what had come after to recognize what was left of the aboriginal world, since even the tropical plants and trees, fruits and crops, had come with the slave plantations and overlaid the mangrove swamps of the early days, he was also starting a new life that was to be launched and funded by his history of *El Dorado*. He woke from his dream of hope in New York, where he discovered that his publisher had rejected the book. He found himself in a rented flat in Victoria, British Columbia, with the germ of what later became *In a Free State*:

> Now the idea was all that I had at the moment in the way of writer's capital; and it was touched with the mood of the historical book I had written; my disappointment; and the homelessness, the drifting about, I had imposed on myself. I had as it were – and as had happened often before – become one of my own characters. (*EA*, p. 151)

He was not alone. Among other figures who seem to enter into the chief character of *The Mimic Men*, for example, is Edward Gibbon. The story of the novel could be read as the shift of a Caribbean colony, one that resembles a cross between British Guyana and Trinidad, to independence within the Commonwealth. The new government slides from nationalist politics into racial violence. It could also be read as an earlier stage of decline and fall continued in *Guerrillas*, a story in which erotic and occult fantasy contrasts with the classical prose of the novel's style. The titular central figure, a disgraced but still youthful colonial minister from the island of Isabella, is called Ralph Singh, but he writes with the unsettling poise of the author of *The Decline and Fall of the Roman Empire* and the *Autobiography*. There is even an impish hint, one of several that Naipaul scatters through his work, that encourages this kind of stylistic connection. At the novel's end, as Singh concludes the memoirs we have just read, he includes among his possible futures, 'Or I might spend the next ten years working on a history of the British Empire' (*MM*, p. 251). At the beginning, however, he seems bent on writing an inverted version of Gibbon's self-praise and fulfilment. While Gibbon stresses how fortunate he has been, how sheltered from the barbarism and slavery of others, Singh declares that he has been cast away, prematurely finished, by just those consequences of his colonial history – now organized as a political force. Gibbon celebrates 'the evening of life':

> I shall soon enter into the period which, as the most agreeable of his long life, was selected by the judgement and experience of the sage Fontenelle. His choice is approved by the eloquent historian of nature, who fixes our moral happiness to the mature season in which our passions are supposed to be calmed, our duties fulfilled, our ambition satisfied, our fame and fortune established on a solid basis.[15]

Singh at once echoes and parodies this in setting himself so prematurely to the composition of his work of self-assessment and reflection on the times:

> These are not the political memoirs which, at times during my political life, I saw myself composedly writing in the evening of my days. A more than autobiographical work, the exposition of the malaise of our times pointed and illuminated by personal experience and that knowledge of the possible which can come only from a closeness to power. This, though, is scarcely the book to which I can now address myself. True, I write with composure. But it is not the composure I would have chosen. For, far from being in the evening of my days, I am just forty; and I no longer have a political career. (*MM*, pp. 7–8)

The poised rhythms and reflective tone are perfect and absurd, at once out-dated and precocious. Gibbon's plummy satisfaction with his garden and library, his vanquished critics and refined acquaintance among the patricians of Lausanne; all this is rewritten as Singh's Parthian withdrawal into his hotel on the outskirts of London, where every prospect displeases and memory mocks both present and past.

67

Singh is now far from his Roman villa on Isabella, from his Loeb edition of Martial, from his brief rule after the departure of the battalions, from the tribal killing, the stones webbed by hair and blood. He is in oblivion, displaced to the imperial capital that for him, in a further wicked reversal, is the greatest void of all:

> The career of a colonial politician is short and ends brutally. We lack order. Above all, we lack power, and we do not understand that we lack power. . . . Once we are committed we fight more than political battles; we often fight quite literally for our lives. Our transitional or makeshift societies do not cushion us. There are no universities or City houses to refresh us and absorb us after the heat of battle. For those who lose, and nearly everyone in the end loses, there is only one course: flight. Flight to the greater disorder, the final emptiness: London and the home counties. (*MM*, p. 8)

Part of what is being mimed here, as Hobbesian phrases ('short and ends brutally') seep into the Gibbonian periods, is the arch and allusive jargon that Singh learned earlier at what sounds very like the London School of Economics. The use of 'transitional' is another token of this inverted style, which Singh attributes to Sandra, the fellow-student who later became and ceased to be his wife, 'She spoke of workmen as "operatives"; she often linked unconnected sentences by "with the net result that . . .", my two-roomed flat became our "establishment", for which there had to be "catering". Perhaps it was the influence of the School' (*MM*, p. 48).

Singh's edgy sensitivity to style, his discovery that the colonial masters themselves may have a numb or fumbling grip on the language and literature they conferred on their subjects, is part of Naipaul's larger and exacerbated sensitivity to how people tell their stories as well as to what stories they tell. In *The Enigma of Arrival*, where the colonial narrator and his patrician are linked by both the literary language and the memory of the British Empire, the narrator is fascinated by the Edwardian affections of his landlord's speech as well as by his literary pastiches, by the way he pronounces 'peony' and 'balcony' to chime with 'pony'. More satirically, the narrator notices the malapropism of a local who describes his political allegiances. Falling somewhere between 'out-and-out' and 'downright', he wonderfully calls himself a 'down-and-out Tory' (*EA*, p. 221). One of the more unexpected after-effects of imperial decline and fall is that the subject may be left with a better command of the language than his sometime master. This can become a joke, and Naipaul satirizes the comic correctness of the native's speech as well as the sloppiness of his master's. He had read and seems to have enjoyed Max Beerbohm's parody of Conrad, which is a mockery of both as well as a send-up of the novelist's overwritten style. As master and man wait for customers to emerge from the jungle on their cannibal isle,

> There came from those inilluminable depths the equable rumour of myriads of winged things and crawling things newly roused to the task of killing and being killed. Then detached itself, little by little, an insidious sound of a drum beaten. This sound drew more near.
> Mr Williams, issuing from the hut, heard it, and stood gaping towards it.
> 'Is that them?' he asked.
> 'That is they,' the islander murmured, moving away towards the edge of the forest.
> Sounds of chanting were a now audible accompaniment to the drum.
> 'What's that they are singing?' asked Mr Williams.
> 'They sing of their business,' said Mahamo.
> 'Oh!' Mr Williams was slightly shocked. 'I'd have thought they'd be singing of their feast.'
> 'It is of their feast they sing.'[16]

The dialogue of this parody echoes as it were in advance the satirical parodies of Naipaul's early West Indian fiction. And there is more than a trace of his unwearying disillusion in Beerbohm's parody of Conrad. The satirical side of Naipaul's prose style creates and confirms a vision of the world like that of the last days of the Hapsburg Empire, a situation that is desperate but not altogether serious.

Underlying Singh's Augustan tones and satirical wit are other voices, other dialects; sometimes conflicting, more and more prophetic of violence and dread. Ralph Singh, whose name was self-invented out of Ranjit Kripalsingh, tries to pass off the name his parents gave him as part of a larger enigma — '"Ranjit is my secret name", I said. "It is a custom among Hindus of certain castes. This secret name is my real name but it ought not to be used in public"' (*MM*, p. 94). This, as his schoolmaster points out, leaves him anonymous, which is what he says he wants. But his deeper secret and inward language is derived from the name 'Singh', which means 'warrior'. He reads *The Ayran Peoples and Their Migrations* and out of this book fashions a dream vision in which he is both the pale horseman and the conquering rider, so that he embodies the racial dream about their origins that underlies so much of Hindu culture and caste and his own fantasy that he is their lost leader, cast away on the island of Isabella.

In his fantasy, which Naipaul the traveller evoked earlier in *An Area of Darkness* and returned to much later in the cold heights above the Kaghan valley in *Among the Believers*, Singh says,

> I lived a secret life in a world of endless plains, tall bare mountains, white with snow at their peaks, among nomads on horseback, daily pitching my tent beside cold green mountain torrents that raged over grey rock ... I was a Singh. And I would dream that all over the Central Asian plains the horsemen looked for their leader. (*MM*, p. 98)

Freud's concept of the family romance, which is based on this fantasy of a noble but unacknowledged birth, is here retold by Singh in a narrative that reveals as it conceals his other secret story and narrative, the untold story of which he is the hero. And yet this story has to be told in the degraded and dangerous conditions of Isabella, where racial politics based on different myths give Singh a rather different role. Like his black ally Browne — a wordplay that we are meant to notice — Singh speaks the dialect of the people as he advances to power and its sudden loss. This part of the novel overlies or doubles another narrative, the historical account of the rise and sudden fall of Cheddi Jagan – in what was then British Guiana – that Naipaul offers in *The Middle Passage*. And this account is personal as well as historical. He stayed with and came to know both Jagan and his wife; he retells not only their story but also the way they told that story themselves, even the way Cheddi Jagan switched back and forth between patois and the language of the study or council chamber. And yet that too is a history he can only allude to and cannot retell.

He is reduced to writing what seems at first to be a *Bildungsroman*, a raffish tale of his student days in London. But realism quickly yields to a sequence of ritual meditations on the life he has lost. That life in turn revolves around the partly told story of the life and violent death of Singh's father, who developed into and died as a Hindu fanatic, leader of a cult that parodies Singh's fantasies about his Aryan origins among the horsemen of the high Asian plains. We will turn in the next chapter to the obsessive metaphors of taboo and defilement that recur in this story and throughout Naipaul's writings: 'taint' and violation are the words repeatedly used to describe both Singh's fantasies and his life. But the narrative itself becomes transformed into an analogue or translation of this family romance. The story of Singh's father becomes entangled with the story of his friendship with the creole Deschampsneufs, lordly enough to speak dialect to their inferiors, rich enough to own some of Isabella's best race-horses. All of these stories are haunted by a question that comes out of the void and recurs with ever greater urgency to Ralph Singh: *'Why, recognizing the enemy, did you not kill him swiftly?'* (*MM*, p. 81). This question, which at first seems an enigma, receives a terrifying response in the disappearance and ritual killing of Tamango, the finest horse in the stable of the Deschampsneufs:

It was more than death. A charcoal burner had found the animal, garlanded with marigold and faded hibiscus, on a freshly prepared platform of beaten and plastered earth.

71

Heart and entrails had been torn out; but there were flowers on the animal's mane, flowers woven into its tail. . . . Banana suckers had been planted at each corner of this smaller platform; and at each corner a swastika had been traced out in flower. *Asvamedha*: to myself alone I spoke the word. It filled me with unexpected awe and horror. An ancient sacrifice, in my imagination a thing of beauty, speaking of the youth of the world, of untrodden forests and unsullied streams, of horses and warrior-youths in morning light: now rendered obscene. My mind, at once literal and fantastic, created a picture of a deepening, endless tunnel: into this I felt I was ever descending, when all I wanted was to return to the light.

The killing of Tamango was inevitably linked with my father and his followers. (*MM*, p. 140)

The secret history of Singh's origins, of the Aryan horsemen and their pure cool world, is retold not once but three times, and each time the allegory reveals something about the book Singh wanted to write but cannot, about the historian he wanted to become.

Taken in turn, these retellings turn the book's narrative into metaphor, the unwritten history into myth. The migrations of the Aryan peoples turn into the corrupted ritual killing of the race-horse. The Deschampsneufs, owners of the horse, have through their migration to Isabella and their miscegenation of French and African blood, parodied a second time Singh's untellable history. *Their* fantasy about origins is related to another book, to Stendhal's novel *Le Rouge et le noir*, which they read as a piece of family history. They apply to an ancestor – said to have gone as a girl from Santo Domingo to Paris, where she became infatuated with Stendhal – a few sentences in creole dialect that Julien addresses to the Marquis de la Mole. Although doubts occur to him later, Singh is at first convinced by a family romance that shames his own:

I was deeply impressed. I felt that Mr Deschampsneufs's story had brought the past close. It was possible to believe in the link between our island and the great world. My own dreams were rendered absurd. The outside world was stripped of its quality of legend and reduced to the comprehensible. Grand figures came near. A writer accounted great had been turned into a simple man, fat and middle-aged and ironic. And nearness exalted; it did not diminish. (*MM*, pp. 174–5)

This second version of family romance has a meaning for Singh that becomes his own story, what a reviewer might offer as the plot of *The Mimic Men*. Even this third allegory starts from a metaphor already identified in a book, once again in *Le Rouge et le noir*. After hearing their story, and in saying good-bye before leaving Isabella for England, Singh is mortally offended by Deschampsneufs, who turns a blind eye to his attempt to shake hands. Singh recalls the question 'Why, recognizing the enemy, did you not kill him swiftly?' and then, as though out of the blue, he thinks back to his reading of the novel:

Our attention in class had been drawn to Stendhal's cleverness in making Julien, right at the beginning of the book, mistake water on a church floor for blood. This had seemed to me crude. But now, full of the closeness of Stendhal, I looked at the red sky and saw blood. And yet was glad I was leaving. Do not dismiss melodrama and style: they are human needs. How easy it is to turn that landscape, which we make ordinary by living in it and becoming part of it, into the landscape and the battlefield. (*MM*, p. 176)

Both metaphors are mistakes, considered as acts of perception; but if we take them as allegories, both are prophetically true. And what they prophesy are the narratives that lie ahead. Julien's water seen as blood foretells his own early death, and Singh transfers or translates this metaphor, whose 'melodrama and style' he recognizes, into the killing that lies ahead for his island, the violence that will drive him into exile.

Even this multiple retelling does not exhaust Naipaul's drive to engrave one narrative on top of another. We have already seen how the narrative of *Guerrillas* retells a documented crime that itself arose from and was enacted through fictions and rituals. Both *Guerrillas* and *The Mimic Men*, for all their clarity

73

on the surface, are troubled farther down, as though something or someone had been dragged down to the bottom and not yet settled into stillness. Their stories are much more opaque, even enigmatic, than they are usually made to seem, and their violence is like that of an underwater struggle – all the more unsettling because of the displaced medium in which it takes place. This clouding and upheaval in *Guerrillas* and *The Mimic Men* surfaces in the reading of the narrative, where the displacement from one story to another is sometimes elliptical, even crytpic. The repeated question ('Why, recognizing the enemy') is hard to trace to a source, not only because it refers to more than one narrative but also because Singh, like Salim later in *A Bend in the River*, is a character who embodies several characteristic ways of speaking, some of which go beyond or fall outside what might seem to be the limits of their consciousness or power to express it. Like Santosh in 'One out of Many', they say more than they seem to know. As Singh reflects on the killing of Tamango, the ancient name of sacrifice, *Asvamedha*, comes into his mind, but he does not say it aloud to be heard by others: 'to myself alone I spoke the word'. This inward speaking of sacred words, this submerging of certain parts of stories – all this is related to the presence and evocation of Naipaul's Hindu and Brahmin ancestry. And that in turn is related to the floating past that he returned to the West Indies to find or invent. The last journey that Singh made before leaving Isabella for England as a student was to visit his father, now renamed like his son, but with the Hindu name of Gurudeva. The family likeness goes beyond the fact that both have renamed themselves. Naipaul's own father, who was meant to be a pundit, entitled his book of stories after the longest of them, *Gurudeva and other Indian Tales*. And the character of Gurudeva, Naipaul tells us, was 'based, remotely, on some one who had married into my mother's family but had then been expelled from it, the mention of his name forbidden' (*AG*, p. 20). One story more that hides another, and behind that story the shadow of caste, the search for purity that is a flight from defilement, sacred words and forbidden names. The corruption of ritual sacrifice in the killing of Tamango pulls Singh down into an Indian world that he had imagined to be light and serene, nobler than the makeshift world of Isabella, but that now seems to him a heart of darkness; a feeling of violation that pervades this novel and a great part of what Naipaul has written.

# 4

## TRAPDOORS INTO A BOTTOMLESS PAST

> Literary description always opens onto another scene set, so
> to speak, 'behind' the this-worldly thing it purports to
> depict. (Michel Beaujour, 'Some Paradoxes of Description')

If Naipaul's West Indian world and its history comes to seem a
makeshift fantasy, writing about it forces him to recognize
other worlds that make new claims on his consciousness. These
worlds, which turn into visions as he writes about them, cluster
around three areas and themes. The first and earliest is the
world of India, especially of Hindu ritual, and the vision of
illusion he creates out of and within that world – the dream of
unravelling cloth that implies the undoing of the universe. This
world was closest to his early life; it lay around him in his
infancy, but its full significance only became clear to him as he
wrote about his travels to the subcontinent in *An Area of
Darkness, India: A Wounded Civilization*, and several of
the essays that were later republished in *The Overcrowded
Barracoon*. This vision retrospectively influenced his fiction set
in the West Indies, especially *The Mimic Men*, and reappears in
*In a Free State, Guerrillas*, and *A Bend in the River*, where it
breaks the surface as acts and fears of defilement or as sexual
loathing. The second of these visionary areas is the world of
Islam, whose fundamentalist revival – the subject of *Among
the Believers* – has spread what Naipaul views as a tidal wave
of fanaticism and the rejection of civilization across Asia and
into parts of Africa and the New World. It would be a mistake
to interpret this vision as anti-Arab, as a form of racism: most
of the people he talks to and wonders at from Teheran to
Java are not Arabs, and he recognizes the conquering energy
of the early caliphs as comparable to that of the Spanish

conquistadors in *The Loss of El Dorado*. But it would not be a mistake to see it as an attack on what Naipaul considers brutal and parasitic superstition based on a bogus interpretation of history.

A premonition of this vision had appeared earlier in the documents and fictions that centre around *Guerrillas*, in the fantasies of Black Power that claimed Moslem origins. The violence with which societies and individuals can turn against civility and reality is one of the chief subjects of the essays on Argentina and Uruguay in *The Return of Eva Perón*. Its other fictive form, as we shall see, is the divided consciousness of characters in *A Bend in the River*, corrupted by gadgets and weapons taken over from a civilization they do not understand. The third and most recent of these visionary worlds appears in the 'plateaux of light', the historical past of England and Rome that the narrator of *The Enigma of Arrival* creates out of the landscapes, houses, and people he returns to live among. He returns out of the other worlds of his books, however, and each stage of his life in that Wiltshire countryside, including its beginnings, is directly related to a crisis in his writing career. And his meditations on England and Rome, so closely identified with his own life and prose style, circle repetitively and then cyclically around images of decline that become intimations of his mortality and confrontation with death.

What it might mean for a character to be a Hindu, and even more, to be a Brahmin, enters only slowly into Naipaul's fiction. At first it seems to be only play:

> Mr Biswas had never questioned the deference shown him when he had gone to Tara's to be fed as a Brahmin and on his rounds with Pundit Jairam. But he had never taken it seriously; he had thought of it as one of the rules of a game that was only occasionally played. (*HMB*, p. 70)

And yet the fantasy of the Aryan horesemen 'riding to the end of the world' that Ralph Singh sees as changed into something obscene by the killing of Tamango according to Hindu ritual is itself, as Naipaul had discovered in India, a Hindu fantasy. Part of his larger discovery of himself as a writer could even be said to lie in his recognition that realism can be transformed into ritual in any society that lacks or does without the shared codes or rules on which realism depends. What is true of a society becomes true of the fictional character. In the midst of seducing girls during his student days in London, for example, Singh reflects on behaviour on his part – keeping a written record of his triumphs, keeping stockings, 'various small garments' and even a pair of shoes – that might have been more pathological than playful. 'The warning signs were so clear. Yet at the time I thought I was simply playing, that in the keeping of trophies and writing-up of experience I was expressing a non-existent side of myself. As though we ever play' (*MM*, p. 26). That last thought has the unexpected insight that hints at an implied author jogging the narrator's pen.

It is the author and writer who tells the reader, in the Foreword to *India: A Wounded Civilization*, about the revelation he has gained in India about the rituals of his earlier life in Trinidad:

The customs of my childhood were sometimes mysterious. I didn't know it at the time, but the smooth pebbles in the shrine in my grandmother's house, pebbles brought by my grandfather all the way from India with his other household goods, were phallic emblems: the pebbles, of stone, standing for the more blatant stone columns. And why was it necessary for a male hand to hold the knife with which a pumpkin was cut open? It seemed to me at one time – because of the appearance of a pumpkin halved downward – that there was some sexual element in the rite. The truth is more frightening, as I learned only recently, near the end of this book. The pumpkin, in Bengal and adjoining areas, is a vegetable substitute for a living sacrifice: the male hand was therefore necessary. In India I know I am a stranger; but increasingly I understand that my Indian memories, the memories of that India which lived on into my childhood in Trinidad, are like trapdoors into a bottomless past. (*IWC*, p. 10)

This prose underplays the revelation at hand by postponing it, increases its meaning by reading his ignorance back into childhood. The growth and delay in understanding is directly tied to the book we are about to read ('as I learned only recently, near the end of this book'), a prevision that is like the author's clairvoyance about the soldiers who will later try to find their way home to Egypt through the hot sand of the desert at the end of *In a Free State*.

This is literary description as Michel Beaujour describes it in the epigraph to this chapter: it opens 'onto another scene set, so to speak, "behind" the this-worldly thing it purports to depict'. And its quality as prose depends in great part, as does Naipaul's style throughout, on a fastidious ellipsis that makes our glimpse through the trapdoor at once memorable and irrevocable. He never tries to outwrite the wonder of his subject. His narrative strategy, like that of the ethnographer, lies in touching the pitch of superstition without being defiled by it. Before I had read anything by Naipaul I came upon and read Nirad Chaudhuri's *The Autobiography of an Unknown Indian*, one of the great books of our century, and through it caught a different glimpse of the animal sacrifice that Naipaul alludes to through his description of the pebbles and pumpkin – that are themselves symbols of that sacrifice. Chaudhuri's description of a buffalo sacrifice of the Bengali Hindus in his ancestral village 'To the pleasure and victory of Mother Durga' shows how different the glimpse might have been:

> The scene was the same as at the goat sacrifice, but instead of the familiar priest there stood that singularly handsome old man, with the scimitar uplifted in a trembling hand. He waved it for a moment, and then brought it down like a guillotine on the neck of the animal.
>
> The scene which followed seemed like an orgy even to those of us who were inured to these scenes. All the servants, all the spectators, all my relatives, old, middle-aged and young, fell on the convulsive and, as it seemed to us, mountainous carcass of the buffalo, smeared themselves and the others with its blood, and pelted one another with the mixture.[17]

Naipaul writes about Chaudhuri, who is one of the few writers about India he admires, in two essays republished in *The Overcrowded Barracoon*. In the second of these essays, whose title is significantly 'The Last of the Aryans', Naipaul joins Chaudhuri in citing a story from the Hindu epic, the *Ramayana*, that shows the racial cruelty and unending defilement that provoke the kind of sacrifice they describe and allude to. The story illustrates Hindu abhorrence of the aboriginal inhabitants of India, known to Chaudhuri as 'the Darks':

> It is reported one day to Rama, the Aryan hero, that the son of a Brahmin has died suddenly. There can be only one explanation: an act of impiety. Rama goes out to have a look and, sure enough, finds that a young Dark has been performing Aryan religious rites. The Dark is at once decapitated and the Brahmin's son comes back to life. In later versions of the story the Dark dies happily: death at the hands of an Aryan is a sure way to heaven. Not even slavery created so complete a subjection. (*OB*, p. 74)

These Aryan fantasies, which Naipaul condemns as the basis for what he describes as 'Hindu apartheid', may be the hidden source for Singh's fantasies about his origins: Naipaul's essay first appeared in 1966, the year before *The Mimic Men*. In a more pervasive way, his two books and several essays about India gain depth and force by endlessly rewriting and contradicting the travels and stories of earlier writers – Kipling, Gandhi, Narayan, among others – just as his books about the West Indies grapple with Ralegh, Trollope, and Froude. In creating and disowning his ancestors, trying to overcome what he describes as 'the Hindu sense of exile and loss' (*OB*, p. 75), he has written in a way that meets Harold Bloom's definition of a fully imagined work as a 'ratio between texts', as an attempt to deal with his writing ancestors by writing them into his own work: his father, the author of *The Adventures of Gurudeva*, was to be the first of many.

The strain in his Hindu ancestry that most excites and resists his attempts to write about it, so much so that it has become a spoor traceable in all his work, is the dread and sense of pollution, of defilement. Singh's first reaction to the ritual killing of Tamango expresses his feeling that *he* has been defiled by it: 'what I next heard . . . gave me more strongly than ever the sensation of rawness and violation: rubbery raw flesh, tainted holy oil' (*MM*, p. 140). In remembering his Trinidad childhood, Naipaul recalls with surprise that others were less sensitive to dietary taboo than his family was. Others would eat from plates on which they had earlier served food for their pets; other children would share their sweets and popsicles. The double function of forbidden or unclean things that are taken in at the mouth is first to defile and then, when swallowed as expiation, to purify. Chaudhuri argues in his *Autobiography* that this shows how far Hinduism has been reduced to fetishism, and how much eating has to do with the reduction. His nephew tells him of the expiation forced on a man whose cow was accidentally strangled by its tie-rope:

> To begin with, he had to go into sackcloth, drink half a glass of bovine urine, and fast for one day. For the next three days he had to live and sleep in the open on the spot where the cow had died, and also to abstain from eating anything but plain rice unseasoned even with salt.(*Autobiography*, p. 437)

And yet such a reduction of morals to eatables and fetishes also has to be seen as an expansion of superstitions until they become all-important. Chaudhuri brings this out by asking his nephew what *wrong* means:

> Without a moment's hesitation he replied that it was *sin*. Then I asked him how men could make amends for any wrong done by them. He replied, 'By expiation'. 'What is expiation?' I finally inquired, and got the expected, in fact the inevitable reply, 'Eating something'. What he had in mind was of course the eating of cow-dung, which forms an indispensible part of most Hindu expiatory rites. (*Autobiography*, p. 438)

In his travels through India Naipaul responds as Chaudhuri does to this fantasy of purity. He goes further in noticing how

81

the fantasy extends to the other orifices, allowing at one and the same time casual excretion and fastidious codes of bathing, the lechery of the *Rig Veda* or erotic sculpture and Mahatma Gandhi's hysterical chastity. Neither Naipaul (nor Chaudhuri before him) has been forgiven for this critique of Hinduism, nor for presuming to judge an ancient culture by the standards of civilized enlightenment. Never more so than when he turns witty over what appals him, as in parodying Churchill's war-time words to account for India's omnipresent excrement: 'Indians defecate everywhere. They defecate, mostly beside the railway tracks. But they also defecate on the beaches; they defecate on the hills; they defecate on the river banks; they never look for cover' (*AD*, p. 70). What appals him is not only the defiling fact but also and even more the blind eye that Indians turn to it, a blindness that itself arises 'out of the Indian fear of pollution', a refusal to admit what contradicts a symbolic order that has displaced reality to become a cruel illusion.

In Naipaul's fiction the eye that sees defilement never closes. Even the servant Santosh preserves the Aryan racial dread of the dark-skinned, even among the blacks of Washington, and after doing the act of darkness with one of them he tries to cleanse himself of the stain. Bathing, rubbing his penis with half a lemon, howling on the floor in tears, and finally fashioning a dhoti for himself out of cloth he has brought from India so that he can try 'to meditate and become still' (*IFS*, pp. 38–9) – all this in a comically horrible sense of self-pollution that is at once racial and sexual. There is nothing comical and much that is horrible in the turn this double revulsion takes in *Guerrillas* and *A Bend in the River*. In both, sexual relations that are also racial relations turn to misogynist violence. In *Guerrillas*, Jane's fantasies about Jimmy's blackness tempt her to a last assignation that ends with her violation and death. More disturbing even than this outcome is the snake-eyed revulsion of the narrative that leads up to it. It is the narrator who notes one after another details of her body, dress, and gestures that make her less an object of desire than a source of pollution: the period spots around her mouth, the way she touches herself, even her nakedness: 'Against the rest of her the red, aged skin below her neck looked like a rash; the little folds of flesh in her shaved armpits were wet' (*G*, p. 237).

Not long before writing *Guerrillas*, in 'The Return of Eva Perón', Naipaul dwelt on the twist of Argentine *machismo* that made anal sex the test of male power. This twist, along with the details we have seen from 'The Killings in Trinidad', enter into the anal rape and cutlass slashing that close this climactic part of the narrative. From her entrance into the novel, and even before that through flashbacks, Jane is described as 'the violated' and made the counterpart as well as victim of the men in her life and death; each of whom in turn is marked by sexual inadequacy. D. H. Lawrence once said that every murderer requires a murderee. Here it would seem that every sense of pollution requires its source. The liaison of Salim and Yvette in *A Bend in the River*, which begins in the white light of his painted windows, turns to his violent disgust. He beats her black and blue, then spits between her legs.

Throughout all of this revulsion there is a precision and pleasure in language linked by metaphors and phrases to the revulsion itself. In a description of Yvette's beauty and its lessening, for example, Salim speaks of 'the wasting asset of her body'. And in a scarifying scene earlier in the novel, Salim's friend Indar, like him an Indian from the coast of Africa and the man who urges the need to trample on the past, recounts the day he went up to London from somewhere like Oxford to find himself a career as a diplomat. The country of his choice – 'since a diplomat has to have a country' – is India. Then follows a visit to India House that is like a miniature of Naipaul's travel narratives. So too is the High Commission a miniature and microcosm of the country it represents. An attempt made in one office after another to fend off Indar's outrageous request, to treat him as an outcast – in several senses – is a masterful piece of writing. The story it bitterly tells of the outcast trying to find his lost homeland is repeated through his attempt to find the right office, some trace of recognition or welcome. As he rises higher in the hierarchy the photos of Gandhi and Nehru contradict the meanness of the bureaucrats he has to deal with. What completes and might be said to start the brilliance of the observation is Indar's own caste consciousness about those he meets. 'His name was the name of his merchant caste', for example, or 'he had probably taken the name Verma to conceal his caste origins' (*ABR*, p. 153). He finally faces someone of importance, 'a fat black man in a black suit . . . He reeked of caste and temple, and I was sure that below that black suit he wore all kinds of amulets' (*ABR*, p. 154–5). But he wants nothing to do with Indar, this 'man of divided loyalties', and tells him to tough it out in Africa. The encounter ends with Indar, closing the circle of caste, colour, and taint, saying to himself: 'For himself the purity of caste, arranged marriage, the correct diet, the services of the untouchables. For everybody else, pollution. Everybody else was steeped in pollution, and had to pay the price!' (*ABR*, p. 155).

The shadows of taboo that stretch across Naipaul's narrative do not always show the figurative precision of this passage. Sometimes the notion of violation or pollution remains just that, vague and sketchy, and we wonder why the Caribbean around Isabella – to take one example among many – should be so insistently described as 'the tainted sea'. But the longing for purity that lies, or once lay, behind this sense of defilement shapes both the fantasies of his characters and the themes of his recent novels and works of reflection. This shaping force works negatively in his rejection of this longing for purity as a falsifying of human history even more strongly than as a positive temptation toward Himalayan snow or the clean deserts of Araby; temptations that his imagination continues to entertain and yield to. This double pull toward and away from, a reciprocal and mythic translation between the imaginative life and the history of peoples, explains the interplay between fictions and histories throughout his writing life. It also helps to explain the great attempt of his most recent work, *Among the Believers* and *The Enigma of Arrival*, to write himself into mankind's history. As James Joyce set himself to work on *Finnegans Wake* in 1922 he explained his intentions to Harriet Weaver by saying, 'I think I will write a history of the world.'[18] Naipaul's history, like Joyce's, can only be written by transcending traditional modes of writing, this time on the level of subject rather than on the level of style. And his transformed subject is a history of empires rewritten as a history of visions and dreams, from the conquistadors' dream and desire for 'the complete, unviolated world' to the 'plateaux of light' in *The Enigma of Arrival*. It is a history that begins with the rise, decline, and fall of Rome and its Empire (which provides part of its style and resonance) and continues through the collapse of the British Empire and the revolt of Islam.

The boldest claim of purpose in Naipaul's expanding history appears in an epigraph to *Among the Believers*, a passage from Polybius' account of the rise of Rome:

> Now in earlier times the world's history had consisted, so to speak, of a series of unrelated episodes, the origins and results of each being as widely separated as their localities, but from this point onwards history becomes an organic whole: the affairs of Italy and Africa are connected with those of Asia and of Greece, and all events bear a relationship and contribute to a single end. (*AB*, p. 6)

Polybius, an expatriate Greek exiled to Rome by the Roman masters of his homeland, half-prisoner, half-guest of the state and its more cultivated leaders, devotes his life to writing a history of the world. And it is precisely the rise of Rome, a spread of civilization that has eclipsed the power of his native Greece and of many other lands as well, that has made this new universal history both possible and necessary. Possible because it tempts the mind, necessary because it consoles the spirit, of the defeated Polybius. Like the ancient idea of fate, it leads the willing and coerces the unwilling. Naipaul may have savoured some of the parallels between his attempt and that of Polybius; not only the scope of the work but also its modernity, its attempt to narrate the world that was rising around him and toppling the old order. There was nothing ancient or archaeological about the history of Polybius. Large parts of it were recent or current events, and his methods of research and writing were similar to Naipaul's in *Among the Believers*: travels, reading, interviews with participants and eye-witnesses. And like Polybius, Naipaul had seen the coming of his history in his own time: he found himself writing the history of his age, even of his own life.

The first stage in this new history, *Among the Believers*, has a theme he had seen emerging over a period of years. Several years before the return of Khomeini to Iran and the creation of a theocratic state by the Ayatollahs, Naipaul had begun to comment on the resurgence of Islamic fanaticism that this change in Iran brought to the world's attention. In his Foreword to *India: A Wounded Civilization*, for example, he notes the renewal, in great part through new economic power, of the spread of Islam, and raises the issue of conquest that became a theme in the later book:

> Arabia, lucky again, has spread beyond its deserts. And India is again at the periphery of this new Arabian world, as much as it had been in the eighth century, when the new religion of Islam spread in all directions and the Arabs — led, it is said, by a seventeen-year-old boy — overran the Indian kingdom of Sind. (*IWC*, p. 7)

And in *A Bend in the River*, as Salim reflects on the many Arabs he sees in the parks and streets of London, he suddenly has a revelation, sees a revenant from his own past on the African coast:

> I saw an Arab lady with her slave. I spotted the fellow at once. He had his little white cap and his plain white gown, proclaiming his status to everybody, and he was carrying two carrier bags of groceries from the Waitrose supermarket on the Gloucester Road. (*ABR*, p. 241)

Salim carries his news home to Nazruddin, who is about to become his father-in-law. Nazruddin has been reflecting on the wider implications for the future of an expansion and migration which both he and Salim are estranged from and yet apparently part of:

> I'm superstitious about the Arabs. They gave us and half the world our religion, but I can't help feeling that when they leave Arabia terrible things are about to happen in the world. You just have to think of where we come from. Persia, India,

Africa. Think of what happened there. Now Europe. (*ABR*, p. 242)

The travels that take Naipaul from Iran to Indonesia in *Among the Believers* bring home to him the vast scale and mobility of Islamic fundamentalism, its renewed spread to the east and south. He has moments of serenity among the communities that gather together from a dozen countries to meditate and pray, often out on the edge of great deserts, among what Naipaul calls in Pakistan 'the salt hills of a dream'. He conducts a long and increasingly acerbic series of interviews and conversations with those who may be able to explain the meaning of this new propagation of the faith; to explain or reconcile its demand for Islamic justice and freedom with the cutting off of hands, the exclusion of minorities like the Chinese in Malaysia, and above all, the puritanical diatribes against a western civilization that is still expected to offer its products and enlightened decencies to societies that in theory want to have nothing to do with either. It is this hypocrisy, once masked for western audiences, that most arouses him. And it was this hiding of one story or history by another that first drew him to the idea of writing such a book. His discovery, like Salim's near the Gloucester Road supermarket, comes in an unexpected place and way: in Connecticut, watching the television news during the early stages of the Iranian revolution, watching interviews with Iranians living in the United States:

> There was a man in a tweed jacket who spoke the pure language of Marxism, but was more complicated than his language suggested. . . . He was proud of his Iranian revolution – it gave him glamour. But at the same time he understood that the religious side of the revolution would appear less than glamorous to his audience; and he was trying – with the help of his tweed jacket, his idiomatic language, his manner – to present himself as sophisticated as any man who watched, and sophisticated in the same way.

> Another evening, on another programme, an Iranian woman came on with her head covered to tell us that Islam protected women and gave them dignity. Fourteen hundred

87

years ago in Arabia, she said, girl children were buried alive; it was Islam that put a stop to that. Well, we didn't all live in Arabia (not even the woman with the covered head); and many things had happened since the seventh century. Did women – especially someone as fierce as the woman addressing us – still need the special protection that Islam gave them? Did they need the veil? Did they need to be banned from public life and from appearing on television? (*AB*, p. 16)

Those last ironic touches are a reminder that Naipaul had known something of the Muslim world from his life in Trinidad and thought it had no claim on his interest or attention: 'The glories of this religion were in the remote past; it had generated nothing like a Renaissance. Muslim countries, where not colonized, were despotisms; and nearly all, before oil, were poor' (*AB*, p. 16).

The man in the tweed jacket and the woman in the *chador* excite a certain malice in the narrator for another and more personal reason. The man is described as having a certain glamour – a word that Naipaul in other contexts applies to the writer, at times to himself. There is a hint here, if not of imagined rivalry, then of comparison and evaluation. Like Indar at India House, he casts a cold eye on those who try to mask the truth about their origins or about their purposes, especially when they do so in front of a western audience. And the woman too, not only because her appearance on television is forbidden her by the fundamentalism she projects, but also because, from an Iranian novel he read at about this time, Naipaul would seem to have got an explanation of her strange attitude. The heroine in the novel seems to have explained the 'angry nun' on the screen. The heroine is a youngish Iranian woman settled in Boston, a biologist married to an American scientist. A holiday return to Iran turns, through a story Naipaul analyses in detail, into her renunciation of her American life, husband, research, Boston, everything, and her decision to put on the *chador* and all that implies. Naipaul sees this vehement taking up of Shia Islam as 'an Iranian death pact'

(*AB*, p. 19). That novel's heroine interprets the other veiled self seen on television, a fiction unmasks another story that turns out to be a fantasy. And that is explicitly how Naipaul reads the novel: 'People can hide behind direct statements; fiction, by its seeming indirections, can make hidden impulses clear' (*AB*, p. 17). With or without other documents, stories, or accounts, this is how he reads or hears the autobiographical sketches he elicits from the people he meets, most of whom are educated or make some claim to sophistication and experience of the larger world outside Islam: doctors, journalists, wing commanders, poets. Part of the intensity of these travel accounts, in this like what Naipaul himself calls the 'obsessive' pieces that earlier made up *The Return of Eva Perón*, lies in the way they rival a possible but unwritten fictional account. And the need to unmask gives even greater value to this way of writing history as a mode of reflective fiction.

A poet met in Jakarta, Sitor Situmorang, is not an invention of the narrator's, but his story, which Naipaul calls 'Reconstructing the Past', shows why the history narrated here may soon be lost beyond recall. Sitor is not only a poet: he was also committed to Sukarno's side in the military seizure of power that led to the killing of many hundreds of thousands of communists, one of the most fanatical massacres in modern history. Sitor emerged from ten years in jail and began to write again. Since he had never known his parents, his past was a void; a void filled by a Canadian woman anthropologist who took him back to his village in Sumatra and explained to him a tribal life, his own life, that he otherwise could never have known. This is beyond irony; and it could also be said that Naipaul's account of his literary and political life offers to another audience an account that would otherwise not be known, or even knowable. That anthropologists alone can create or recreate the pasts of peoples and individuals whose lives, richly funded by memory and custom, they were originally supposed to record, is a mode of reconstruction similar to Naipaul's, and we shall in closing see how much the ethnographer's ways of writing resemble his. Sitor's ability to say, 'This is how my ancestors lived for eighteen generations', and to say of himself 'I am complicated. But not confused' (*AB*, p. 295) depends upon the memory of others. But Sitor, as Naipaul reveals, is no simple victim or man whose life has had a happy end: 'He now possessed his ancestral village, the valleys, the lake, the stone walls, the fairy-tale houses. But he could no longer go back there; he couldn't pretend to be what he had ceased to be' (*AB*, p. 296). Without European interest in his poetry and in his 'complication', his life within and between cultures, he would be lost; just as Naipaul would have been had he been caged within a West Indian audience and culture.

After his release from prison Sitor met and married – according to his own rediscovered tribal rites – a young Dutch woman whose work in Indonesia is to encourage the craft skills in rattan, reed mats, and baskets: a cultural role that is the converse of Sitor's. This twist in the meaning of Sitor's life does not exhaust the discoveries we are meant to make in reading Naipaul's account of it. Although estranged, like several other members of his family, by reading and education from tribal life, Sitor is the son of a chief; and after ten years in prison he had to be re-initiated into his tribe. But even this ceremony threatens to go terribly wrong, chiefly through the 'complications' that made it necessary in the first place, and Naipaul's sensitivity to taboo and sacrilege refines his description of it:

> For this ceremony the skull of his grandfather was taken out of the stone sarcophagus with the lizard of good luck carved on the lid. Sitor held a plate with this skull and a lemon, the lemon an agent of cleansing. There was a cousin of Sitor's at the ceremony. The cousin was a medical man, and he saw that the lower jaw of the skull had slipped while it was being transferred to the plate for Sitor. He reached out and put the jaw back in place. The shaman or priest was furious. The cousin, by touching the ancestral skull, threatened to undo all the good and to bring bad luck on them all. (*AB*, pp. 292–3)

The anecdote verges on allegory. The knowledge of anatomy, the western medical science of the cousin, threatens to undo the rite made necessary by Sitor's defilement in that other world, by his plunge into poetry, revolutionary politics, and jail. As a final revelation, through Naipaul's belated reconstruction of Sitor's *other* erased past, we learn that under Sukarno he had become a politician and man of power as well as a poet, a man still unforgiven by many of those whose careers he had damaged. The novelistic richness and 'complication' of this narrative make it a document out of which Naipaul could now write a subtler sequel to *The Mimic Men*; though it could also be read as an extended allusion to the earlier novel. The way in which Naipaul shapes his account around Sitor's attempt to write his autobiography looks forward to the palimpsest of reconstructed pasts in *The Enigma of Arrival*. There the writer's life and his meditations on it lead him to overlay one misunderstood or mysterious character or history on top of another until a true account of his life emerges. The resulting account is profoundly romantic, a life comparable to Wordsworth's *Prelude*, in which the initial void of the self expands through writing until it fills the universe.

# 5

## PLATEAUX OF LIGHT

> In their lowest servitude and depression, the subjects of the
> Byzantine throne were still possessed of a golden key that
> could unlock the treasures of antiquity, of a musical and
> prolific language that gives a soul to the objects of sense, and
> a body to the abstractions of philosophy. (Gibbon, *Decline
> and Fall of the Roman Empire*, LXVI)

Naipaul's most recent works, especially *Finding the Centre* and
*The Enigma of Arrival*, seem to slip outside the usual modes of
writing and yet to be suffused with the light and voices of other
writers, other books. They are at the same time echo chambers
of his own life of writing, repeating themes and phrases that at
first spread outward like sound or shock waves from a single
'good sentence' or from a visionary glimpse of the world within
him. His history of the world begins in a primordial sense of
loss and estrangement, as unarguable as Wordsworth's and
expressed in almost the same words: 'The history I carried with
me, together with the self-awareness that had come with my
education and ambition, had sent me into the world with a
sense of glory dead; and in England had given me the rawest
stranger's nerves' (*EA*, p. 52). On first reading his earlier books
and talking to others about their way of bridging between
fiction and history, I noticed their resemblance to romantic
prose, where the writer's self is both the bridge and the traveller
between these worlds and ways of writing. I was thinking of
De Quincey's *Confessions of an English Opium Eater*, for
example, where the visionary dream, the 'sense of glory dead'
and the 'myriads of accusing faces' all seemed to be elements
these writing selves had in common. At other times, especially
in following Naipaul into his essays or on his travels, I was

reminded of the energy and purpose of Lamb's *Essays* and Cobbett's *Rural Rides*. In *The Enigma of Arrival* and in an essay published since he has celebrated these writers and acknowledged their presence in his work. In what follows I want first to look more closely at this allusive relation; then, taking a step back, to trace some telling affinities that his narratives bear to the writings of anthropologists. Not just to the restructuring of pasts that would be lost without them, but also to those autobiographical supplements like Malinowski's *Diary in the Strict Sense of the Term* or Lévi-Strauss's *Tristes tropiques*. Then in closing, I want to step sideways to compare the remarkable tone of Naipaul's prose with that of some other writers, mostly American, who share with him the power to *underwrite* the disorder and poignancy of the world. He is in the end, and has been almost from the start, one of those writers who convey intensity not by raising but rather by lowering their voices; who give a new dimension to fiction by seeming to undercut its claims. Naipaul to my mind stands and rises to greatness as a writer because his prose has such precision and strength. His feeling for language, his mastery of style, show that Gibbon was right. However belated and Byzantine the cultural conditions may be, however sunk in servitude and depression, the discourse of literature can still restore to the human spirit what might otherwise seem lost beyond recall.

Naipaul's growing empathy with a romantic spirit of place and distance can be traced through his growing feeling of closeness to Conrad. That feeling was very different from any liking for the clotted prose and heavy breathing over significance that marks much of Conrad. He is less than impressed by Conrad's creative imagination, in which he finds something 'flawed and unexercised'. And yet he both quotes and shares Conrad's declaration: 'The romantic feeling of reality was in me an inborn faculty' (*REP*, p. 202); even more, he devotes most of his essay to a precise analysis of what this statement means in Conrad – and of what it means to him. In Conrad, and in his own words, this feeling of reality arises from subjects and themes that were all he had, over which he had no choice and little control. The passage in which Conrad explains himself could, allowing for some stylistic shifts, be read as an *apologia* for the writer who quotes it:

> I have a natural right to my subjects because my past is very much my own. If their course lies out of the beaten path of organized social life, it is, perhaps, because I myself did in a sort break away from it early in obedience to an impulse which must have been very genuine since it has sustained me through all the dangers of disillusion. But that origin of my literary work was very far from giving a larger scope to my imagination. On the contrary, the mere fact of dealing with matters outside the general run of every day experience laid me under the obligation of a more scrupulous fidelity to the truth of my own sensations. (*REP*, p. 202)

What is renounced matters as much as what is claimed, and Conrad's forced choices foreshadow Naipaul's. To write about lost outposts and islands in air because you have abandoned 'organized social life' and been excluded from it; to trust to an impulse that only shows itself to be genuine in retrospect, and after many lost illusions; to be forced into 'scupulous fidelity' and away from fantasy or free play of the imagination precisely because your world is outlandish and already at an end of the imagination; all of this was later admitted and asserted by Naipaul about his own writing life. He was in fact returning to one of the primal impulses in romanticism, the impulse to set free tongues tied or silenced by oblivion and oppression, to bring inside the circle of culture, to bring up to one of the 'plateaux of light', the outcast or despised or unrecognized. And since that had been his early fate, as it had been Conrad's before him, Naipaul discovered that the disturbing thing about romanticism is not that it is false, but rather that it comes close to being true.

This discovery is one of several that Naipaul made in settling into his cottage on the shrunken estate in Wiltshire, the centre around which *The Enigma of Arrival* turns. It is a discovery he makes chiefly through walks and books that explain and interpret what he sees and wonders at on those walks:

These beeches were at the edge of the farmyard, big trees now in their prime, their lowest branches very low, providing a wonderful, rich, enclosing shade in the summer that made me think of George Borrow and his wanderings in *The Romany Rye* and *Lavengro*. (*EA*, p. 83)

But some of his most surprising discoveries are made by talking and reflecting on the people around him. Here too books interpret people who would otherwise be enigmas, but they are different books, written by angrier writers from a standpoint that is in every way closer to romantic radicalism:

He hated titled people and old families and people of inherited wealth in a way I wouldn't have thought possible for an English person, until I read William Cobbett. There, in the prejudices and strongheadedness and radicalism of one hundred and fifty years before, a radicalism fed by the French Revolution (which in the pages of Cobbett, in the living, breakneck speed of his prose, could still feel close), I found many of the attitudes of Bray. An empire had intervened, a great new tide of wealth and power; but the passions of Bray were, miraculously, like the passions still of a purely agricultural county, the passions connected with manors and big farms and dependent workers. (*EA*, p. 222)

Here again a trapdoor into the past, but one that is no longer bottomless. The past that he comes to grasp through Cobbett about the man standing in front of him is historicized and already part of his meditations on the ending of the British Empire.

And there may be an even closer connection between what Naipaul noticed on his walks and what Cobbett recorded on his *Rural Rides*. They are, for one thing, writing about the same place, about the rich valley of the Wiltshire Avon. This valley, and the contrast between dilapidated or vanished manors and vast new farms, fine crops and herds set against famished farmers and herdsmen, was the occasion of some of Cobbett's angriest and most poignant outbursts. What the valley of the Avon showed to him was an earlier stage of the agricultural

revolution that Naipaul encounters after it has transformed the
landscape and its people, no longer famished, but oddly root-
less among so many rooted things; men and women who are
full of surprising newness and an old unappeased desire for
dignity. They turn out to be, most of them, as much strangers as
Naipaul himself, as much part of the huge migrations of
peoples, the *Völkerwanderungen* since the Second World War,
that Naipaul perceived as one of the great themes for modern
literature and began to narrate in *In a Free State* and *A Bend in
the River*. His Wiltshire neighbours have come shorter dis-
tances, but for many the sense of displacement is total. Naipaul
even displaces echoes and responses from Africa to Wiltshire,
seeing the hills of Africa around, hearing in the servile defiance
of a boy who has been loutish on the bus – 'Sir?' – the tones of
an African servant – 'Bwana?' – or the even more mocking
'Massa' with which Jimmy closes *Guerrillas*. The story that
Naipaul has to tell about this landscape differs in important
ways from the narrative that developed out of Cobbett's
visitations, and yet they have in common an expectation of
dereliction, a narrative of glory dead. They dwell on the fading
or falling into ruin of the manor, and there may even be a hint
to Naipaul in the way Cobbett describes this change and the
transformation of gardens that goes with it:

> This Netheravon was formerly a great lordship, and in the
> parish there were three considerable mansion-houses, be-
> sides the one near the church. These mansions are all down
> now; and it is curious enough to see the former *walled
> gardens* become orchards, together with other changes, all
> tending to prove the gradual decay in all except what
> appertains to *the land* as a thing of production for the distant
> market.[19]

The two writers respond in very different ways to this dereliction: against Cobbett's anger we recognize Naipaul's tempered
pleasure. He realizes that his own presence there is a sign of
how far the manor has fallen. And yet he grasps at a sense that
his presence is a fulfilment, or even perhaps more, of the
deprivations of his indentured ancestors:

To see the possibility, the certainty, of ruin, even at the moment of creation: it was my temperament . . . . Possibly, too, this mode of feeling went deeper, and was an ancestral inheritance, something that came with the history that had made me: not only India, with its ideas of a world outside men's control, but also the colonial plantations or estates of Trinidad, to which my impoverished Indian ancestors had been transported in the last century – estates of which this Wiltshire estate, where I now lived, had been the apotheosis. (*EA*, p. 52)

Even the words lie light as paper on the ground: 'estate' or 'plantation' in Trinidad meant something mocked by this lordly estate, just as Negro slaves in the West Indies were often given the names of Hannibal or Caesar. Deeper than the landscapes and the words lies the role of romantic prose essays, travels, pamphleteering, autobiography, naturalist observation in undoing throughout *The Enigma of Arrival* the structure and conventions of fictive prose, in walking away from the novel.

Soon after the book appeared in early 1987, Naipaul published an essay in the *New York Review of Books* explaining what he had done and what several early nineteenth-century prose writers had contributed. Although the dust-jacket calls it 'A Novel' and the title-page refines this to 'A novel in five sections', some reviewers were not persuaded. Anthony Burgess, appealing to Flaubert, argued that the novel is a complicated contraption, 'a triumph or failure of artifice', and 'there is nothing of artifice about Naipaul's new book!'[20] He likes and admires what he has read, but responds to it the way a watch-maker might respond to a sun-dial. He may have been right to be unpersuaded, because Naipaul's essay makes it plain that he too considers it something very different from the novel as we know it. His argument, which reveals toward the end that it is about his new book, becomes a critique of a novel as a genre that starts from a much more sweeping notion of artifice than Burgess's. To Naipaul the writing of any 'imaginative book', like his own desire to be a writer, is artificial, and the novel is burdened with narrative and plot that we can now do without. Then, with a quick jump at the way cinema and television have speeded up and changed our expectations, he goes on,

> And the nineteenth-century English writers who now give me the most 'novelistic' pleasure – provide windows into human lives, encouraging reflection – are writers who in their own time would not have been thought of as novelists at all.
>
> I am thinking of Richard Jefferies, whose essays about farming people carry so much knowledge and experience that they often contain whole lives. Or William Hazlitt. Or Charles Lamb, concrete and tough and melancholy, not the gentle, wishy-washy essayist of legend. Or William Cobbett, the journalist and pamphleteer, dashing about the country-side. . . . All of these writers would have had their gifts diluted or corrupted by the novel form as it existed in their time. All of them, novelistic as they are in the pleasures they offer, found their own forms. (*NYRB*, 23 April 1987, 7)

What drives him back to these writers is the originality they achieved in the form of their writings, an originality he wants to achieve in his turn. This is being original in a way we are coming to understand through modern literary theory. Originality might even be defined as influence or allusion the reader has missed. And didn't Stravinsky once say that progress in music was a matter of taking two steps *back*?

Naipaul's second move toward originality arises from his misgivings about the differences and confusions concealed under any fictional vocabulary that requires him to use words as though they mean the same thing to his readers and *their* tradition as they do to him, as in the example we have just seen of 'estate' or 'plantation'. His solution, whose first steps he carried out as early as *The Mimic Men* and *The Loss of El Dorado*, he now presents as a bolder move:

> I felt that truly to render what I saw, I had to define myself as writer or narrator; I had to reinterpret things. I have tried to do this in different ways throughout my career. And after two

years' work, I have just finished a book in which at last, as I think, I have managed to integrate this business of reinterpreting with my narrative.

This alteration in the vocabulary of the text, and even more, in the way the narrator or writer must change the usual understanding the reader has of the words, goes back beyond Joyce's *Portrait* to an even more fundamental romantic text, to Wordsworth's *Preface* to the *Lyrical Ballads*. There is even a heroism in Naipaul's decision to do without narrative and plot that is comparable to Wordsworth's argument against any distinction between the 'language of prose and metrical composition'.

We might end this reading of romantic prose in Naipaul where we began, with Conrad. In defining the purpose of his turning away from the nineteenth-century novel of society and manners, Conrad said that his attempt to write about remote or exotic subjects required him to maintain 'a more scrupulous fidelity to the truth of my sensations'. And in explaining his purposes in *The Enigma of Arrival*, Naipaul lays the same stress on fidelity to experience that makes the writer what he is: 'My aim was truth, truth to a particular experience, containing a definition of the writing self.' What though *are* these experiences of the writing self, and why do its narratives alternate or oscillate between documents and fictions?

A possible answer may lie in the repeated fact that these narratives alternate around the same subject and that they usually come in pairs. The principle or occasion is usually the same. Naipaul travels to the West Indies, or to Zaire, or to India, and writes an extended and highly personal account of his travels. Not long after the publication of the travel book or enquiring essay a novel or story appears, set in what is recognizably the same place and emplotted through incidents from the first account. The fictions are often enacted by characters who strikingly resemble persons, many given their actual names, who have already been described, analysed and at times satirized in the travel writing. This is the paired relation, as we have seen, that links *The Mimic Men* with *The Middle Passage*, *Guerrillas* with 'The Killings in Trinidad', parts of *In a Free*

*State* with *An Area of Darkness, A Bend in the River* and 'A New King for the Congo'. In the course of reading these paired narratives I was struck by their resemblance (and their contrast) to what has become virtually a genre in anthropology, the pairing of the ethnographer's personal narrative – often a history of his or her adventures and calamities – with the impersonal or 'objective' account that becomes the contribution to scholarship. Two of these pairings, by Claude Lévi-Strauss and Bronislaw Malinowski, have already been mentioned. Anyone who reads the personal accounts of their fieldwork will I think be struck by the way they foreshadow Naipaul's travel books, or rather by the way his seem to reverse theirs. Lévi-Strauss, as he sails among Europeans to South America, is full of irony and satire that falls away from him as he encounters the numinous world of myth and the schematic patterns of kinship in Brazil. Malinowski's *Diary in the Strict Sense of the Term* is steeped in self-questioning, boredom, malice, and erotic reverie, none of which emerge in his epically entitled *Argonauts of the Western Pacific*.

We have now seen enough of Naipaul to recognize how fully his narratives are a reversal of this pattern. In his earlier enquiries and personal narratives he is sardonic and unillusioned about the exotic and primitive, which to him often have only the dubious charm of the *déjà vu* or even more dubious claims to innocence or wisdom; and yet he is by contrast confident, even credulous, about the values of the western world he has espoused and out of which, as he often has to explain, he has come. While the white anthropologist constantly faces the problem of his visible difference and separation from the darker-skinned people he tries to be accepted among, Naipaul's problem is that of his likeness, the danger that he will be confused with the people he lives and travels with. Not only and obviously in India, but also in many parts of Asia, Africa, and even South America, where he can pass for a native or be confused with the Indian traders and merchants long resident there. A further, and for some of his critics an unforgiveable, aspect of his attitude is his conviction that he already understands and even sees through the society he has entered. Having lived in the cultural and racial micro-cosm of Trinidad, (as we saw in his suppositions about Islam, Africa, and India) he thinks that he already *knows*. This confidence, based upon second-hand acquaintance in a client culture, may be misplaced twice over, but it imparts a tone to his personal narratives that is radically different from what we encounter or overhear in reading the narratives of ethnog-raphers.

The relations of Naipaul's writings with those of the anthro-pologists whose paths he so often crosses assume a pattern if they are seen as part of a growing awareness that ethnography itself is, after all, a way of writing that has styles and a poetics of its own.[21] Mary Louise Pratt, who has looked closely at the questions raised by the pairing of accounts by anthropologists, has noticed certain features of this temptation to retell description and narrative that we might bring to bear on Naipaul. She notices first that 'professional, scientific ethnography' takes great pains to distance and distinguish itself from 'older, less specialized genres, such as travel books, personal memoirs, journalism. . . . This strategy of defining itself by contrast to adjacent and antecedent discourses limits ethnography's ability to explain or examine itself as a kind of writing.'[22] Naipaul's writing points up this blind spot in modern ethnography, all the more so since his personal narratives, like those of many anthropologists, are cast in the despised mode of travel writing. Even worse, Naipaul's travel books are sadly lacking in the piety toward the primitive that marks ethno-graphic work. His more critical essays and books could even seem a throwback to a narrative stance that anthropology has been dedicated to stamping out. Pratt quotes Malinowski's declaration that this had been achieved by the time he came to write *Argonauts of the Western Pacific* in 1922. 'The time when we could tolerate accounts presenting us the natives as a distorted, childish caricature of a human being are gone. . . . This picture is false, and like many other falsehoods, it has been killed by Science' (p. 27). It would be a caricature of Naipaul in turn to suggest that this is how he writes about natives wher-ever he finds them. His description of a village in Indonesia

101

centred around the cult and culture of 'the rice goddess', for example, is admiring and deeply moving:

> To enter one of those villages was to find more than shade. It was to enter an enchanted, complete world where everything – food, houses, tools, rituals, reverences – had evolved over the centuries and had reached a kind of perfection. Everything locked together, as the rice-fields just outside, some no more than half an acre, fitted together.
>
> Every house, with concrete walls or walls of woven bamboo strips, stood in shade; and every tree had a use, including the kapok, new to me. There were many kinds of bamboo, some thick and dark, almost black, some slender and yellow with streaks of green that might have been dripped by an overcharged brush. These bamboos made beds, furniture, walls, ceilings, mats. But rice ruled. It was the food and the cause of labour; it marked the seasons. In the traditional house there was a small room at the back of the pillared main room; this small room, in the old days, was the shrine-room of the goddess Sri, Devi Sri, the rice goddess. (*AB*, p. 320)

His admiration extends to the people who developed and maintained this culture. But what is moving about this passage and this culture is the extent to which it is threatened by what Naipaul regards as a regressive threat, by Islamic fanaticism that may sweep away a syncretic culture balanced between Christian, Hindu, and Muslim beliefs and customs.

His travel writings have a value that anthropologists could recognize along with the common reader. A book like *Among the Believers* tells a story that we did not expect to hear and probably do not want to hear, a story of sectarian violence and zeal that traces the roots of what might otherwise seem unintelligible disasters: the rule of the Ayatollahs, political struggle in Pakistan, the long agony of the war between Iran and Iraq. This story is part of Naipaul's history of the world, of a world undoing itself, but it is also for that reason a world that is descending from the plateaux of light into an ethnographic world, a world without history. The absence of history is not innocent primitivism, not memory as an alternative to written records. History is being killed through a forced oblivion, as Naipaul shows in discussing attempts made in Pakistan to erase historical accounts of the Arab conquest of the Hindu kingdom of Sind. And after the erasure, to show nothing but contempt for the fallen kingdom and its culture; for 'The time before Islam is a time of blackness: this is part of Muslim theology' (*AB*, p. 134).

We come to recognize that this world and Naipaul's paired narratives are finally a reversal of ethnographic writing. His personal or travel account is meant to accompany a novel, not an impersonal description. And the final paradox, as we have seen, is that for Naipaul, the novel never lies: 'People can hide behind direct statements; fiction, by its seeming indirections, can make hidden impulses clear' (*AB*, p. 17). Several years earlier, in reading 'Malik's primitive novel' as a pairing and foretelling of 'The Killings in Trinidad', Naipaul put it even more plainly: 'An autobiography can distort; facts can be realigned: But fiction never lies: it reveals the writer totally' (*REP*, p. 67). A fiction may reveal a murderous fantasy or a complex vision of reality, but to Naipaul it always tells the truth. And it does so for reasons that bring us back once again to the 'romantic feeling of reality' he shares with Conrad. The talented writer who has been excluded from what Conrad called 'organized social life' must be true to his particular experience or to his sensations because that is all he has; the fantasist because he cannot help himself. From other points of view the results are very different; from the perspective of truth they are the same. This view of fiction's relation to truth links Naipaul to certain other writers and to a certain vision of the world.

Before we turn in closing to these writers and to this vision, however, we should recognize yet again how little room or value Naipaul assigns to the imagination. He clearly recognizes the power of impulse and obsession, but not what Freud among others considered the role of imagination in masking impulse and obsession through fables and figures. 'The "work" of the imagination', as Philip Rieff has put it, 'is to distort, complicate, individualize, and thereby conceal the potent sub-individual wishes and desires.'[23] From Naipaul's point of view the imagination does nothing and has no work to do.

Wallace Stevens's paradox – that even this absence of imagination had to be imagined – helps to account for the precision of Naipaul's style, but it also accounts for that style's obsessive refusal of excess, its willingness to repeat what is after all the truth, its *underwriting* of a world that has already been written about as fiction or history. The last pages of *A Bend in the River* narrate Salim's escape from what threatens to be a massacre of all those who can read and write, all the masters and all the servants: 'They say it is the only way, to go back to the beginning before it's too late. . . . They say it is better to kill for days than to die forever' (*ABR*, p. 284). Not at first sight a subject that lends itself to understatement; and yet on second thought the subject *requires* underwriting if the reader and the end of the novel are not to collapse into a horror that would stifle any response. And this is how Naipaul does it. Salim leaves the doomed town on a river steamer (the President's men have taken all the seats on the plane) that evokes Marlow's boat in *Heart of Darkness*. Toward dusk natives in dugouts try to escape with the steamer by lashing their boats to it, then night begins to fall:

> It was in this darkness that abruptly, with many loud noises, we stopped. There were shouts from the barge, the dugouts with us, and from many parts of the steamer. Young men with guns had boarded the steamer and tried to take her over. But they had failed; one young man was bleeding on the bridge above us. The fat man, the captain, remained in charge of his vessel. We learned that later. (*ABR*, p. 287)

The indirection of this description, the way in which its violence is only explained later, when it has become part of history as a report or explanation, echoes the disorder around them. But it also echoes the attack on Marlow's boat, the threat from the banks and the barge: one story tells another. The next and final paragraph of the novel completes this parable of abandonment by repeating several details from earlier episodes, but in the repetition they become metaphors as well as details:

104

At the time what we saw was the steamer searchlight, playing on the river bank, playing on the passenger barge that had snapped loose and was drifting at an angle through the water hyacinths at the edge of the river. The searchlight lit up the barge passengers who, behind bars and wire-guards, as yet scarcely seemed to understand that they were adrift. Then there were gunshots. The searchlight was turned off; the barge was no longer to be seen. The steamer started up again and moved without lights down the river, away from the area of battle. The air would have been full of moths and flying insects. The searchlight, while it was on, had shown thousands, white in the white light. (*ABR*, p. 287)

The barge going adrift, its passengers imprisoned and unaware, the water hyacinths that signify an end to navigation, the searchlight that abandons them all to darkness, the obscure skirmish and the desertion – all of these details leave the story behind as a metaphor. At the very end, the recessional of the verb tenses slips away into more remote pasts – 'would have been full . . . had shown thousands' – and the meaningless life that disappears in the dark after fading 'white in the white light'. Over all and governing all is the calm precision with which the worst is implied and suspicion is confirmed. The clarity with which all the details are noted and ordered makes us aware of the expanding void, the final disorder.

Light that will show us the dark, darkness that will show us the plateaux of light. This is what Naipaul's prose enables us to see, this is what some other writers in our time have shown to us through different ways of underwriting their stories, leaving unsaid or understated what we finally understand. There is an enigma in this that is much greater than the puzzles presented by writers like Joyce or Proust, who overwhelm us with a fullness of detail, an excess of light. This is more like Beckett's later writing, which becomes more expressive by saying less. The Romans used to play on words to say that a grove of trees (*lucus*) was named after light (*lux*) because the light did not shine there: *lucus a non lucendo*. And when Naipaul meditates on the menace of the classical Roman world suggested to him by the de Chirico picture in *The Enigma of Arrival*, it is the clarity of that scene that deepens its mystery and danger. Out of this image of 'a sunlit sea journey' he makes a story, as we shall see at the end, of the writer's life and death; just as he made stories out of the documents he examined in order to write *The Loss of El Dorado*: 'The historian seeks to abstract principles from human events. My approach was the other; for the two years that I lived among the documents I sought to reconstruct the human story as best I could' (*EA*, p. 94). Among modern writers who have played off documents and stories in such an invasive and yet controlled way, I think of Joan Didion, whose novel *Democracy* circles around the Pacific rim and around lives that lead into and away from the fall of Saigon in 1975. This sign of the decline of the American Empire is also a crisis in the lives of the novel's characters, one of whom, with a backhanded wave at the opening of *Moby Dick*, says 'Call me the author' and identifies herself as Joan Didion.[24] Her account of fictitious lives is precise, dated to the minute, day, year; exact about the history their lives share with the headlines in newspapers; and it repeatedly calls the reader's attention, as does Naipaul in *The Enigma of Arrival*, to the novel it is not:

> You see the shards of the novel I am no longer writing, the island, the family, the situation. I lost patience with it. I lost nerve. Still: there is a certain hour between afternoon and evening when the sun strikes horizontally between the trees and that island and that situation are all I see. Some days at this time one aspect of the situation will seem to me to yield the point, other days another. I see Inez Christian Victor in the spring of 1975 walking on the narrow beach behind Janet's house, the last sun ahead of her, refracted in the spray off Black Point.

And the book goes on as 'shards', circling around events and selfconsciously repeating itself to create a 'novel' that parallels many of the techniques that emerge in *The Enigma of Arrival*, though the tone is more edgy and elliptical. What seems to provoke, in both books and in both writers, the dissolution of the novel is the attempt made to rewrite it as a history of our times. This is an attempt that reveals a void to Naipaul; a void at the centre of history that can only be filled through writing that takes the writer and his work as its subject and theme.

In reinterpreting the de Chirico picture that hangs over *The Enigma of Arrival*, he thinks of it at first as a story that would be a rhapsody, a stitching-together of classical literary and religious texts:

> I would take pointers from Virgil perhaps for the sea and travel and the seasons, from the Gospels and the Acts of the Apostles for the feel of the municipal or provincial organization of the Roman Empire; I would get moods and the idea of ancient religion from Apuleius; Horace and Martial and Petronius would give me hints for social settings. (*EA*, p. 92)

As this story grows he begins to see it as a version of the novella *In a Free State*, the story he was then writing. But he finally comes to see it in terms of a repeated dream of his own death that would also be a death in the ancient world. We may wonder what kind of dream that might be, this dream of which the writer says quite precisely that 'I was consciously living through, or witnessing, my own death' (*EA*, p. 93). We notice that he will take from Virgil details of 'the sea and travel and the seasons', a source that may resonate through de Chirico's image of the ship, the port, the disguised figures on the quayside.

All of these elements combine in the opening scene of Hermann Broch's extraordinary novel *Der Tod des Vergils* (*The Death of Virgil*). This impassioned meditation, which has remarkable affinities with *The Enigma of Arrival*, begins with the arrival of the Imperial ships that bear both Augustus and the dying Virgil back from Athens into the port of Brundisium. The description, like Naipaul's pointers, comes in part from Virgil's poetry. We might take what follows as a parable; for the death that Naipaul fears in his dreams becomes a confrontation with death and with human history through the death of his sister. Out of his facing and reflecting on death comes Virgil's last vision of a world undoing itself: 'Nothingness filled the void and became the Universe'.[25] And out of his sister's death, which forces him to face his own, Naipaul gains a closing vision of 'life and man as the mystery', and the impulse to remake the world through his writing: 'And it was when, faced with a real death, and with this new wonder about men, I laid aside my drafts and hesitations and began to write very fast about Jack and his garden.'

# NOTES

1   Lionel Gossman, *The Empire Unpossess'd: An Essay on Gibbon's Decline and Fall* (Cambridge: Cambridge University Press, 1981), p. 91.

2   'The Noble Rider and the Sound of Words', in *The Necessary Angel: Essays on Reality and the Imagination* (London: Faber & Faber, 1960), p. 22.

3   See Paul de Man, *The Rhetoric of Romanticism* (New York: Columbia University Press, 1984), p. ix.

4   Norman Cohn, *Europe's Inner Demons* (London: Paladin, 1976).

5   The resemblance to Dickens was noted from the start, but Martin Fido was I think the first to discuss Naipaul's debt to Wells. See his essay 'Mr. Biswas and Mr. Polly', *Ariel*, 5 (October 1974), 30–7.

6   V. S. Naipaul, 'What I Don't Like', *The Times*, 13 July, 1961, 13.

7   Wallace Stevens, *Opus Posthumous* (London: Faber & Faber, 1959), p. 165.

8   Ronald Paulson, *Representations of Revolution, 1789–1820* (New Haven: Yale University Press, 1983).

9   See 'Jacques Soustelle and the Decline of the West', in *OB*, pp. 206–17.

10   op. cit. *The Times*, 13 July 1961, 13.

11   Edward Gibbon, *The Decline and Fall of the Roman Empire*, LXXI: (New York: Modern Library edition, n.d.), III, 863.

12   Claude Levi-Strauss, *La Potière jalouse* (Paris: Plon, 1985), pp. 227–8: my translation, emphasis in the original.

13   See especially the opening chapters of Margaret Mead, *Purity*

and Danger: An Analysis of the Concepts of Pollution and Taboo
(London: Routledge & Kegan Paul, 1976).

14  Quoted in Richard Ellmann, *James Joyce*, new and rev. ed. (New York: Oxford University Press, 1982), p. 578.

15  *The Autobiography of Edward Gibbon* (London: Oxford University Press, 1907), p. 220.

16  'The Feast', in *Conrad: A Collection of Critical Essays*, ed. Marvin Mudrick (Englewood Cliffs, New Jersey: Prentice-Hall, 1966), pp. 14–15. Naipaul mentions Beerbohm's parody in 'Conrad's Darkness' (*REP*, p. 200) and notes that it is based on 'The Lagoon', a story read to him by his father at the age of 10.

17  Nirad Chaudhuri, *Autobiography of an Unknown Indian* (Berkeley and Los Angeles: University of California Press, 1968), p. 65.

18  Quoted in Ellmann, *James Joyce*, p. 537.

19  William Cobbett, *Rural Rides*, ed. George Woodcock (Harmondsworth and Baltimore: Penguin edition, 1967), p. 321.

20  *The Observer*, 15 March 1987.

21  See as an example of this awareness the collection of essays edited by James Clifford and George E. Marcus, *Writing Culture: The Poetics and Politics of Ethnography* (Berkeley and Los Angeles: University of California Press, 1986).

22  Mary Louise Pratt, 'Fieldwork in Common Places', in *Writing Culture*, pp. 27–8.

23  Philip Rieff, *Freud: the Mind of the Moralist*, 3rd edition (Chicago: University of Chicago Press, 1979), p. 126.

24  Joan Didion, *Democracy* (London: Chatto & Windus/The Hogarth Press, 1984), pp. 29–30.

25  Herman Broch, *Der Tod des Vergils* (Frankfurt: Suhrkamp, 1976), p. 453: my translation.

# BIBLIOGRAPHY

## WORKS BY V. S. NAIPAUL

*Fiction and 'Novels'*

*The Mystic Masseur*. London: André Deutsch, 1957; rpt. Harmondsworth: Penguin, 1964.

*The Suffrage of Elvira*. London: André Deutsch, 1958; rpt. Harmondsworth: Penguin, 1969.

*Miguel Street*. London: André Deutsch, 1959; rpt. Harmondsworth: Penguin, 1971.

*A House for Mr Biswas*. London: André Deutsch, 1961; rpt. Harmondsworth: Penguin, 1969.

*Mr Stone and the Knights Companion*. London: André Deutsch, 1963; rpt. Harmondsworth: Penguin, 1973.

*A Flag on the Island*. London: André Deutsch, 1967; rpt. Harmondsworth: Penguin, 1969.

*The Mimic Men*. London: André Deutsch, 1967; rpt. Harmondsworth: Penguin, 1969.

*In a Free State*. London: André Deutsch, 1971; rpt. Harmondsworth: Penguin, 1973.

*Guerrillas*. London: André Deutsch, 1975; rpt. Harmondsworth: Penguin, 1980.

*A Bend in the River*. New York: Alfred A. Knopf, 1979; rpt. New York: Vintage, 1980.

*The Enigma of Arrival*. London and New York: Viking, 1987.

*Nonfiction*

*The Middle Passage: Impressions of Five Societies — British, French*

111

*and Dutch – in the West Indies and South America*. London: André Deutsch, 1962; rpt. New York: Vintage, 1981.

*An Area of Darkness*. London: André Deutsch, 1964; rpt. New York: Vintage, 1981.

*The Loss of El Dorado: A History*. London: André Deutsch, 1969; rpt. Harmondsworth: Penguin, 1973.

*'The Overcrowded Barracoon' and Other Articles*. London: André Deutsch, 1972; rpt. Harmondsworth: Penguin, 1976.

*India: A Wounded Civilization*. New York: Alfred A. Knopf, 1977; rpt. New York: Vintage, 1978.

*The Return of Eva Perón with The Killings in Trinidad*. New York: Alfred A. Knopf, 1980; rpt. New York: Vintage, 1981.

*Among the Believers: An Islamic Journey*. New York: Alfred A. Knopf, 1981; rpt. New York: Vintage, 1982.

'A note on a borrowing by Conrad'. *New York Review of Books*, 16 December 1982, pp. 37–8.

'Writing "A House for Mr. Biswas"'. *New York Review of Books*, 24 November 1983, pp. 22–3.

'An island betrayed'. *Harper's*, March 1984, pp. 61–72.

*Finding the Centre: Two Narratives*. London: André Deutsch, 1984; rpt. New York: Alfred A. Knopf, 1984. (Includes 'Prologue to an autobiography' and 'The crocodiles of Yamoussoukro'.)

'Among the Republicans'. *New York Review of Books*, 25 October 1984, pp. 5, 8, 10, 12, 14–17.

'On being a writer'. *New York Review of Books*, 23 April 1987.

## Bibliography

Hamner, Robert D. 'An annotated bibliography'. In *Critical Perspectives on V. S. Naipaul*. Ed. Robert D. Hamner, Washington, DC: Three Continents Press, 1977, pp. 263–98.

New, William H. *Critical Writings on Commonwealth Literatures: A Selective Bibliography to 1970, with a List of Theses and Dissertations*. University Park: Pennsylvania State University Press, 1975.

Singh, Sydney. 'Bibliography of critical writing on the West Indian novel'. In *World Literature Written in English*, 22 (1983), 107–42.

Stanton, Robert J. 'V[idiadhar] S[urajprasad] Naipaul'. In his *A Bibliography of Modern British Novelists*. Vol. 2 Troy, NY: Whitston, 1978, pp. 621–64.

Mann, Harveen Sachdeva. 'Primary works of and critical writings on V. S. Naipaul: a selected checklist', in *Modern Fiction Studies*, Vol. 30, No. 3, Autumn 1984, 581–91.

## SELECTED CRITICISM OF V. S. NAIPAUL

Blaise, Clark. 'The Commonwealth writer and his material'. In *Awakened Conscience: Studies in Commonwealth Literature*. Ed. C. D. Narasimhaiah. New Delhi: Sterling, 1978, pp. 118–26.

Bondy, François. 'V. S. Naipaul: Der Westöstliche Inder'. *Schweizer Monatshefte: Zeitschrift für Politik, Wirtschaft, Kultur*, 59 (1979), 643–50.

Boxill, Anthony. *Naipaul's Fiction: In Quest of the Enemy*. Fredericton, New Brunswick: York Press, 1983.

Boyers, Robert. 'Confronting the present'. *Salmagundi*, 54 (1981), 77–97.

Cooke, Michael G. 'Rational despair and the fatality of revolution in West Indian literature'. *The Yale Review: A National Quarterly*, 71, i (1981), 28–38.

Cudjoe, Selwyn R. *Resistance and Caribbean Literature*. Athens: Ohio University Press, 1980, pp. 70, 71, 178, 232–44, 271, 272.

Enright, D. J. 'The sensibility of V. S. Naipaul: who is India?' in *Man Is an Onion*. Ed. D. J. Enright, LaSalle, Illinois: Library Press, 1973.

Fido, Martin, 'Mr. Biswas and Mr. Polly'. *Ariel*, 5 (October 1974), 30–7.

Goodheart, Eugene. 'Naipaul and the voices of negation'. *Salmagundi*, 54 (1981), 44–58.

Hamner, Robert D. *V. S. Naipaul*. New York: Twayne Publishers, Inc., 1973.

King, Bruce. *The New English Literatures – Cultural Nationalism in a Changing World*. New York: St Martin's, 1980, pp. 98–117, 221–3.

McSweeney, Kerry. *Four Contemporary Novelists: Angus Wilson, Brian Moore, John Fowles, V. S. Naipaul*. Montreal, Quebec: McGill-Queen's University Press, 1983, pp. 152–95, *passim*.

Miller, Karl, 'V. S. Naipaul and the New Order'. *Kenyon Review*, 29 (November 1967), 685–98.

*Modern Fiction Studies*, Vol. 30, No. 3, Autumn 1984. V. S. Naipaul Special Number.

Morris, Robert K. *Paradoxes of Order: Some Perspectives on the Fiction of V. S. Naipaul*. Columbia, Missouri: University of Missouri Press, 1975.

Nachman, Larry David. 'The worlds of V. S. Naipaul'. *Salmagundi*, 54 (1981), 59–76.

Neill, Michael. 'Guerrillas and gangs: Frantz Fanon and V. S. Naipaul'. *Ariel*, 13, iv (1982), 21–62.

Parrinder, Patrick, 'V. S. Naipaul and the uses of literacy'. *Critical Quarterly*, 21, ii (1979), 5–13.

Rai, Sudha. *V. S. Naipaul: A Study in Expatriate Sensibility*. Atlantic Highlands, NJ: Humanities Press, 1982.

Ramchand, Kenneth. *The West Indian Novel and Its Background*. New York: Barnes & Noble Inc., 1970.

—'The theatre of politics'. *Twentieth Century Studies* (Canterbury, England), 10 (1974), 20–36.

Rohlehr, Gordon. 'The ironic approach: the novels of V. S. Naipaul' in *The Islands in Between*. Ed. Louis James. London: Oxford University Press, 1968.

Swinden, Patrick. *The English Novel of History and Society, 1940–80*. New York: St Martin's, 1984, pp. 210–52.

Theroux, Paul. *V. S. Naipaul: An Introduction to His Work*. London: André Deutsch, 1972.

— 'V. S. Naipaul'. *Modern Fiction Studies*, 30, no.3 (autumn 1984), 445–54.

Walsh, William. *V. S. Naipaul*. Edinburgh: Oliver & Boyd, 1973.

—'Commonwealth literature: context and achievement'. In *Rhétorique et communication*. Paris: Didier, 1979, pp. 315–32.

White, Landegg. *V. S. Naipaul: A Critical Introduction*. London: Macmillan Press, 1975.

Woodcock, George. 'Two great Commonwealth novelists: R. K. Narayan and V. S. Naipaul'. *Sewanee Review*, 87 (1979), 1–28.

—'V. S. Naipaul and the politics of fiction'. *Queen's Quarterly*, 87 (1980), 679–92.